BONSAI

A Beginner's Guide on How to Cultivate and Care for Bonsai Trees

By Akira Takahashi

Table of Contents

INTRODUCTION

Congratulations on purchasing your copy of *Bonsai: A Beginner Guide on How to Cultivate and Care for Bonsai Trees*. I hope that you find this comprehensive guide on how to start growing your own bonsai tree very helpful and informative.

The art of Bonsai has been practiced for thousands of years, and through this book, you will learn about the different types of trees and plants that are ideal for this method of tree design as well as how to choose the best specimen for your own bonsai project.

Most people have an interest in creating their own display of this art, but they have no idea where to begin. This book will guide you through the process step by step so that there is no confusion as you learn new skills and hone your gardening know how. It is loaded with information which will educate you on all aspects of bonsai care as well as how to design your masterpiece over the next several years.

Styling your own bonsai is a dedicated practice which is quite rewarding. You will learn to appreciate this ancient modality on a personal level in your own home or garden. You will have a piece of art to be able to show off to your family and friends as you share your love for your new hobby.

There are specific instructions for the different common types of bonsai as each has unique intricacies and sometimes challenges that can easily be avoided when following the guide within.

It continues to give tips on the most common mistakes that are made by new owners of bonsais and what you should do if any problems with pests, infections, and diseases you may encounter during the life of your tree.

There are several ways which are utilized to sculpt and shape your new masterpiece. I have also decided to share with your visuals of the common styles, some of which are well known and others are more obscure. Studying these examples specimens with the included gallery will help the beginner bonsai gardener to start thinking creatively at potential goals you will have with your individual piece of nature.

There are opportunities to start this hobby throughout the year, but why would you want to wait? The pride you feel when you have created something unique which can be appreciated by many over the decades will be fulfilling. There is no better time to start than now in educating yourself about this beautiful display of nature which can be shared with family and friends as you learn.

There is no better time than now to start on your new hobby which will bring you closer with nature while learning about this ancient art which anyone will be able to accomplish with the help of the guides in this book.

I have made sure that this book is full of useful information which will help you be successful in your new venture, and I do hope that you enjoy reading and learning about this ancient art form.

CHAPTER ONE

HISTORY & TRADITION OF BONSAI TREES

When one thinks about a Bonsai plant or tree, a petite Japanese tree probably comes to mind. However, the art of Bonsai is applied to trees that are deciduous, broadleaf evergreen and conifer. Centuries ago, the Chinese started *"pun-sai"* and it was only for the elite people in society. They would go out into nature and procure the trees and they were originally elegant gifts. Eventually, the art form spread to Japan which expanded the styles slightly.

The concept of bonsai is that it is part of natures which is captured and miniaturized. The thought behind this concept was based in the Chinese Five Agents Theory which includes earth, metal, wood, fire, and water. The idea is the power that is part of the original natural scene is much more potent and powerful when miniaturized. It would contain the same power as the regular sized tree found in nature. This mini version would be then able to be looked upon to meditate on the power within the scene and gain access to the knowledge contained within.

The first specimens that were found for the purpose of pun-sai were thought to be the more grotesque looking but were considered sacred. One reason these trees would have been chosen is that they could not be used for lumber or any other practical use. Also, the shape of the twisted branches and trunks looked similar to yoga poses.

It was not until the art of pun-sai was brought over to Japan that the name changed to bonsai. This was approximately the year of 1800 and it was the way that the Japanese pronounced the Chinese word pun-sai.

In modern times, the layperson envisions only elderly Chinese or Japanese men working on the art of bonsai. However, it is becoming popular with younger generations as there are several landscapes and varieties of bonsai which are easier to care for.

The popularity of styling mini trees in the form of bonsai spread to the West during the 20th century which continued to make this a favorite hobby of countless individuals around the world. The movement was fast forwarded due to a book which was published in 1957 by Yoshimura and Halford by the name of Miniature Trees and Landscapes. It quickly became known as the "Bible of Bonsai in the West" as it melded the traditional methods with the modern world.

The original Bonsai were procured from the wild and took their interesting features due to the harsh elements they were subjected to. Because these plants started to die out due to over cultivation. Now the Bonsai process is being used for nursery and landscape plants.

The art of Bonsai is a growing relationship with the tree that is being worked with. It is a challenge to a caregiver's design and gardening skills. As a result, artistic talent is displayed through the finished product.

Because the Bonsai tree styles are meant to be a representation of a real scene in nature, it is easier to see the resemblance with the taller varieties. Even though the smaller Bonsais are created with the same depictions in mind, they become more abstract ideas as most trees in nature are much larger.

A bonsai is not known by this name until it reaches its full potential. While they are being cultivated and coached, they are known as *potensai* which is literally a Bonsai in training.

The Bonsai trees are able to live longer, arguably, because of the high amounts of attention to the care they receive. All the time and energy that a caretaker puts into each Bonsai adds potential life. The caregiver is the one who monitors pest infestations, doctoring injuries, protection from extreme weather systems, nutritional and water needs and overall health.

Because everything in the landscape is used to portray and specific style, each piece of the tree has a purpose and a story. These can include flowers, cones, fruits, needles, small leaves, foliage pads, twig and branch reformation, surface roots, the interconnection of live and deadwood, textured bark, thick trunks, even including the container itself.

Each has a story and is a puzzle piece to the larger picture of which the caretaker creates over time. Sometimes several years are required to intricately piece together a perfect landscape in the caretaker's mind. You can imagine the dedication, time, energy and effort that goes into such a grand project. The final result is something that will continue to live on potentially for generations depending on the size and continued care of the trees.

Ideally, when the caretaker puts so much effort into creating this perfect masterpiece, others will appreciate these pieces of art as well. The meaning of bonsai literally translates to "tree in a pot" and is also a method of styling a tree, shrub or vine into a specific shape to mimic the same found in nature in an artistic nature. Most bonsai trees that are carefully shaped over years are miniature versions of what is found naturally. Usually, they are formed to look the same as they do in the wild, but sometimes they are also morphed into a different creative shape which is visually appealing to the eye.

A true work of bonsai art is when it does not seem like a human has interacted so closely with this tree but that it looks more it has instinctively occurred. Bonsais are usually put into colorful containers to add to the visual effect of the art, but they can also be planted directly into the ground as a centerpiece for a garden or to add character to a particular space.

The bonsai gardener may have in mind the overall message behind the display they are creating, but it may be viewed differently by other people. This is the beauty of the bonsai art form as it can have different meanings while remaining the same. Then again, bonsais are able to survive for more than a generation, so the gardener's work may never be complete and another enthusiast will need to take on the vision as time goes by. It is possible for a single tree to take on several bonsai styles within its lifetime.

The art of bonsai is a dedicated path in which you will become intimately close with all the aspects of the chosen tree. You will know when something is wrong with your bonsai just like you would know if your best friend is having a bad day. Others see their bonsais much like a child which needs to be molded into the best they can be which takes a great deal of time and energy.

As a bonsai gardener, you take on the responsibility of making sure not only that the tree is happy and healthy but also aesthetically pleasing for others to appreciate the bonsai as much as you. As a case in point, there is a record of a bonsai tree in Japan living for over 800 years. This longevity can be attributed to the face that all their needs are being handled. Because of the relationship the bonsai gardener has with their tree, they will ideally give what the tree requires in the way of any protection from the weather, pests, injuries and of course the basics of nourishment and water.

As time passes, a bonsai gardener sometimes changes their priorities. When they started out, most gardeners have a grand idea of the final result they will work towards with a tree. As the bonsai enthusiast is involved in every aspect of their tree, they may start to push the priority of keeping their tree alive at all costs and put the design on the wayside, especially if a threat to the life of the tree occurs.

The art of bonsai does not have to be a solo adventure. Especially with larger specimens, there can be several people involved in the care of the tree. They would bring different expertise to the table and then all the other people could ideally learn from them. This is ideal for the beginner who is just starting to venture into the world of bonsai. It can be a confusing undertaking at times. However, when there is more knowledge gained about the particular bonsai which is chosen, there are fewer grey areas in how to take care of your particular variety of bonsai.

Chapter Summary

In this chapter we learned

- The art of bonsai started in China thousands of years ago.
- Bonsais are a miniature version of this same tree found in nature and created into a unique masterpiece

- The history of the bonsai and how it has transformed into what we know today.
- In the next chapter, you are going to learn and explore different types of bonsai trees and shrubs.

CHAPTER TWO

TYPES OF BONSAI TREES

The types of trees that can be cultivated using the Bonsai technique are a conifer, broadleaf evergreen, pine and deciduous. The most common trees for beginners are the Juniper and Ficus Bonsai varieties. These will be outlined first and then there will be a comprehensive overview of the different trees that can be used as bonsais which range from beginner to intermediate for those who want a little challenge. Use this list to research about which specimens are you interested in so that you can narrow it down to your first project.

Juniper Bonsai

The other common type of Bonsai that is a brilliant choice for the beginner is the Juniper Bonsai. This is a variety from the cypress family which is evergreen coniferous shrubs or trees. It is also known by the scientific name of Juniperus. Some popular varieties are the Sierra (Juniperus occidentalis), Rocky Mountain (Juniperus scopulorum) and California (Juniperus californica) which are found easily throughout North America. The varieties found in Europe are the Juniperus Sabina (Savin) and the common juniper (Juniperus communis) plants. The other popular subtypes are the Japanese needle (Juniperus rigida), Japanese Shimpaku (Juniperus sargentii), Chinese juniper (Juniperus chinensis) and Green Mound (Juniperus procumbens).

The leaves have a wide range of colors from light green to darker blue-greens which can be needles or scale-like depending on the age of the plant. The subtypes of Juniper that have the needle-like foliage throughout the life of the tree are the Common Juniper, Green Mound, and Japanese Needle Juniper. For the remaining scale-like foliage Juniper Bonsais, they can take a long time to reach their maturity. It takes about 3 years for the juvenile needle foliage to get to the point of being able to be fully removed.

7

There are cones which are oval or berry shaped and can range from 3 mm to 2 cm. These also take approximately 1 to 2 years to ripen. These cones are typically eaten by birds who end up spreading the seeds through their droppings.

The trunk of the Juniper trees is ideal for producing deadwood known as shari or jin. This wood is the result of a dying or broken branch which will dry out and eventually die. The combination of colors that can be seen with these varieties of Juniper is yellow-brown or reddish-brown bark. Coupled with the white deadwood and the green leaves, the Junipers can be a beautiful visual display.

With this being a popular variety of Bonsai, these are found easily in nurseries or can be cultivated from their natural environment. If the caregiver wants to have fast growth, use high nitrogen levels within the fertilizer during the spring months.

It is recommended to transfer the trees every 2 years for younger plants and wait for every three to four years for older Juniper Bonsais. You need to use a soil that drains well to ensure the roots will not be subject to root rot.

Ficus Bonsai

The Ficus Bonsai is part of the mulberry plant family (Moraceae) and is known by the common name of the Fig tree. This is a tree that is to be grown indoors and is by the far the most popular species that beginners first start with. The beauty of this tree is there are hundreds if not thousands of subspecies within the Ficus family. They grow in tropical conditions and are found on all inhabited continents. Because of all of these factors, it makes it very easy to cultivate indoors in a controlled environment.

The most common subtype of the Ficus that is grown is the Ficus Retusa which usually has a trunk that is a curved S and has dark green and oval foliage. The next popular subtype is the Ficus Ginseng which shares many of the same qualities as the Ginseng root which has a thick trunk. The other varieties of the

9

Ficus include Taiwan, Religiosa, Golden Gate, Willow leaf, Tiger bark, and Mircocarpa.

The Ficus leaves have pointed tips which aid water dripping off of the foliage. Depending on the subtype, they start quite small at 1 inch (2 cm) in length or can be as long as 20 inches (50 cm). The bark of the trunks is typically grey and smooth with some varieties such as Tigerbank and Microcarpa showing special patterns. As a note, the Ginseng Bonsai leaves, in particular, can be poisonous for pets so precautions need to be made in case this is true for the situation.

These leaves have pointed tips which aid water dripping off of the foliage. Depending on the subtype, they start quite small at 1 inch (2 cm) in length or can be as long as 20 inches (50 cm). The bark of the trunks is typically grey and smooth with some varieties such as Tigerbank and Microcarpa showing special patterns. As a note, the Ginseng Bonsai leaves, in particular, can be poisonous for pets so precautions need to be made in case this is true for the situation.

Typically, the Ficus trees are rather large with a crown circumference of at least 1000 ft. and have a milky sap with has a latex consistency which seeps from any cuts or wounds in the fig tree. Some types of Ficus have flowers which are hidden in the pods where the fruit grow. These pods are only able to be pollinated by the fig wasps. The fruit-bearing Ficus, such as the Ficus carica, produce purple-blue, red, green and yellow fruits which vary in size from a few millimeters to many centimeters.

It is rather easy to find the Ginseng Bonsai varieties as they are readily available at nurseries and home building supply stores. Although, they do not come without their own problems. They may come with under fertilized soils, unattractive shapes or there may be scarring from improperly grafted branches. Scarring can also result due to wire biting into the bark while it was growing.

If desired, cuttings from the Ficus bonsai can be taken with the highest rate of success during the high summer weeks. If you care to grow them from seed, this works well during the spring months.

This variety of bonsai is very resistant to pests but monitoring is still required throughout the life of the tree. If the Ficus is allowed to be in the dry air, this will weaken the strength of the branches and foliage which will result in the leaves dropping.

When this tree is in this weakened state, it is more likely to be infested with spider or scale mites. Sticks of insecticide which are placed in the soil are helpful in eliminating these pests. During this period, place the plant under artificial lamps for approximately 14 hours each day while misting the leaves through the day to help it recover.

There are many other varieties of trees, shrubs, and vines which can be molded into beautiful bonsai masterpieces. They are divided into Deciduous Tree, Broadleaf Evergreens and Conifers and Pines. Each choice has benefits for the beginner and experienced alike.

Deciduous Tree Bonsais

Chinese Pepper Bonsai

The Zanthoxylum is a popular indoor bonsai which is subtropical. It is also known as the Sichuan Pepper and is native to Korea and Japan. This shrub grows to the height of 6 feet (2 meters) tall and can withstand temperatures as low are 50° Fahrenheit (10° Celsius). It has tiny green-yellow flowers, and the "fruits" that are formed is a Chinese pepper which hot spices can be produced. These peppers are red and look much like peppercorns. This bonsai has glossy and dark green leaves that are paired and compound. The branches and trunk sometimes have thorns which can make wiring a challenging experience.

If the plant is located in a warm climate, it can be kept outdoors throughout the year. For any temperate climate, the shrub can be set in part shade or sunny space which is free from wind from May to September. This bonsai requires temperatures of 60 - 75° Fahrenheit (16 - 23° Celsius) from the fall to spring months. It is important to keep the Chinese pepper out of any cold drafts.

Flame Tree Bonsai

This variety of bonsai is known also by many names such as Delonix regia, flamboyant tree, Royal Poinciana and fire tree. They are originally from tropical areas and have golden or red flowers coupled with the green ferny foliage.

The seed pods grow between 12–24 inches (30 and 60 cm) long and can grow too large if they are not managed. The bark is smooth for the juvenile trees which grows rougher as it matures while maintaining its grey-brown color. As the flame tree bonsai grows quickly, it develops an umbrella shape naturally which makes it ideal for bonsai caregivers.

As for the wintertime, it is necessary to bring the tree inside or to protect against any lower temperatures. The ideal winter conditions for the flame tree are between 50° and 68° Fahrenheit (10° and 20° Celsius).

Because of the tropical nature of the flame tree, an ideal environment is a place outside of the wind that is quite sunny. It cannot withstand any sudden drops in temperature and as such is usually grown indoors in a controlled environment. Note that the longer that the flame tree bonsai is kept in a dark and cool place, the longer it will dormant and not produce foliage.

During the growing season of summer, the flame tree requires a significant amount of water. Still, precaution needs to be headed for not overwatering as this variety suffers from frequent root rot. In fact, it can withstand short periods of dry soil. When the leaves have fallen during the winter months, less water is required. The pH of the soil needs to stay between 4.5 and 7.5 and the water needs to have normal levels of limestone.

The caregiver is going to change out the containers for the flame tree bonsais about every year and replace with soil which drains well which is mixed approximately 25% with Kanuma. Also, the roots can be pruned at the time of transplant up to 30%. Take the opportunity to remove all dead roots as well as the strong roots at the base of the container.

During the winter time, the flame tree bonsai are more susceptible to scale, caterpillars and shoot borer infestations. If this occurs, scrape them off of the plant and then use a pesticide specific to the problem.

Japanese Elm

This native of Taiwan, Korea, and Japan is also known as the Zelkova Bonsai. The most common subtype goes by the name of the Japanese grey bark elm and is more of a classic style of Bonsai tree.

Naturally growing up to 10 feet (30 meters) in height, the foliage has the broom style shape which is a traditional characteristic of Bonsai trees. The trunk is singular which fans out to contain several branches and twigs. Usually, have a smooth and grey trunk, the juvenile twigs are slightly red.

The foliage is dark green during the spring and summer months while transformed to a colorful display of purple, red, orange and yellow during the fall months. The leaves are oval shaped and long having a rough and serrated top while smooth on the bottom. When these elms are potted, the leaf size diminishes considerably from the naturally growing trees.

This variety of Bonsai is tolerant to slight amounts of frost yet need to be protected from extreme exposure to the cold by either being brought inside if grown outdoors or placed into a greenhouse. It can be grown both indoors or outdoors which makes this a fantastic variety for beginners to work with.

The roots will need to be pruned every two to three years when the young elm bonsai is transplanted. The older trees can be reported approximately every four to five years. The soil should be within the range of 5.5 to 6.5 and would be a standard mix.

Pests rarely attack the Japanese Elm except in rare instances. If an infestation occurs due to leaf spots, spider mites, leafhoppers, aphids or gall mites, use a specialized pesticide for the particular situation.

Japanese Maple

Also known as the Acer palmatum, The Japanese Maple is originally from Korea, China, and Japan. There common shrub subtypes of these maples are Seigen, Deshojo, Arakawa, Shishhigashira, Kashima and Kiyohime.

The foliage that is present is typical of the maple leaves which include five points. There is a beautiful range of colors during the spring, summer and fall months which are bright red, orange and yellow.

The trunks vary in color depending on the age of the plant from reddish and green for the juveniles and range from light grey to grey-brown for the mature plants.

They have clusters of flowers which are green-yellow tint and are seen usually between the months of May and June. These flowers then transform into seeds which have two wings.

It is best to re-pot the Japanese Maple every two years while pruning the roots well as the root system can completely fill a pot if allowed. A combination of pumice, lava rock and Akadama is recommended to give the Maple bonsai sufficient draining soil.

Since the Japanese Maples are hardy, they rarely see infections of pests. However, a common pest during the spring is the aphid. Customary insecticide treatments can be used in this case.

A fungal disease known as verticillium wilt is a threat for these bonsai as it can result in at least a partial if not full death of an infected tree. You will know if this is present by the black spots which are observed in the wood at the trunk. If a caregiver notices these spots, they need to disinfect their cutting tools so they do not spread the disease further.

Magnolia Stellata Bonsai

The Magnolia bonsais require a significant amount of sunlight and are best grown outdoors. The only concern for protection is when the temperature dips below 14° Fahrenheit (-10° Celsius) as they are quite hardy. If it is in a container, it needs to be transplanted every two to three years with a standard mix of soil. During the re-potting process, prune back no more than 20% of the root system.

Oak Bonsai

There are many hundreds of subtypes of the Oak bonsais which are generally deciduous with a small amount being evergreen. They are of the Quercus family, and they produce fruits known as acorns. They are found naturally throughout North and Central America, Southwest Asia, North Africa, and Europe. The most common subtypes are the American White Oak (Quercus alba) and the European Oak (Quercus robur).

This variety of bonsai are very hardy and grow as high as 131 feet (40 meters) tall. The trunks can have a thick circumference of 47 inches (120 cm) or more depends on the subtype. The Oak Bonsais have heavy and thick branches which hold the lobed foliage which range from approximately 4 to 8 inches (10–20 cm). The leaves are dark green through the year except when they turn brown and yellow during the fall. Even though they are strong trees, they need attention and protection during the cold winter months.

The Oak bonsais require a space with a decent amount of air movement as well as full sun. When the soil gets to be dry, the oak needs to be watered. However, refrain from over watering and keeping the dirt too wet.

When you are fertilizing the Oak bonsai, keep the nitrogen levels from getting too extreme as this will cause the tree to be more susceptible to mildew and pests as well as produce large leaves. When you transplant every two years, be sure to cut back to the root system no more than 30%.

The biggest threat to the Oak bonsai is powdery mildew. In rare cases, pine-oak gall rust, bacterial leaf scorch, and oak leaf blister affect the foliage. Other pests that can be found are the oak worms, leafminers, scale, and aphids. These usually can be managed with a stream of water to remove them from the tree.

Weeping Willow Bonsai

Out of the hundreds of subtypes that are included in the weeping willow bonsai group are the Salix x sepulcralis (Chrysocoma) and Salix babylonica and Salix alba (Tristis). The typical weeping willow characteristics are the swooping branch coupled with yellow twigs. They originally come from China, but they are common throughout the northern hemisphere.

Naturally, they can grow upwards to 20 meters and can live anywhere from 80 to 200 years when they are properly cared for. The willow bonsais thrive in wet soil which is why they are usually located near rivers, lakes, and ponds.

This would be a more challenging project for a beginner, as it will take a decent amount of energy and patience to see this bonsai tree to full maturity. They grow rather quickly which will need to be controlled as well as require constant and careful watering.

It is ideal to keep the weeping willow bonsai outdoors and keep it as a larger tree as the hanging branches require much space. Even with the larger trees, the shoots of the weeping willow bonsais need to be secured so that it does not grow as tall as it would naturally. The branches can also be finicky as they can die for no particular reason.

If you live in an area where the sun gets particularly hot during the summer, the weeping willow will need a somewhat shady spot to stay during this time period. Otherwise, they thrive in sunny conditions and as such need protection during the winter before the first frost.

Because the weeping willow is typically near a water source, it will require watering several times a day during the summer to keep the soil moist. It is imperative that the soil does not go dry. During the winter time, keep the dirt wet enough to keep the roots from drying up.

The caregiver will know when this variety of bonsai needs transplanted as the buds will start to swell. Typically, the weeping willow bonsai will require a new container each year. Prune the roots as necessary to provide room for expected growth in the new pot. The soil should be a balance between well-draining yet able to retain water. A touch of limestone gravel or pumice combined with the soil should help achieve this balance.

There are several pests which can infest the weeping willow bonsai including canker, gall mites, caterpillars, scale, aphids, willow borer, and gall makers. You can use a pest specific pesticide during these cases.

Wisteria Bonsai

This is a vine which has clusters of alternating leaves which are very fragrant. These are usually grown in gardens over facades or constructed terraces and are found in North America, Japan, and China. There are small varieties of the Wisteria Bonsai with the most popular being Japanese (Wisteria floribunda) and Chinese (Wisteria sinensis). These are the subtypes which create the longest clusters of flowers which make them ideal for caregivers to cultivate for artistic displays.

There is a wide range of colors with the most common being blue-tinted purple, but they can also be dark purple, pink or white. The Wisteria bonsai also produce seed pods which spread the seeds by opening rapidly, forcing the seeds to fall far away from the plant itself. For pets and humans alike, the pods and seeds are poisonous.

The focus of the Wisteria bonsai are the flowers rather than the trunk or branches specifically. The flower clusters consist of most of the plant and cover the branches and trunk considerably to where they are hardly noticed.

These are a longer term bonsai which requires anywhere from 10 to 15 years for a bonsai cultivated from seeds to flower and mature. If you graft or cut the bonsai from another vine, it will reach maturity in approximately 8 to 10 years.

Unless the caregiver wants the foliage to grow more quickly than the flowers, nitrogen levels in the soil need to be kept at normal levels.

Every two years, the caregiving needs to re-pot the wisteria if kept indoors for the juvenile plants. When the vine matures, you can transplant every three to five years. It is best to transfer your plants in the spring before the flower buds start to open. There is no need to prune the roots as the vine tends to be more productive with a mass of roots. The pH level of the soil should be between 5.5 and 6 while using a standard mix of dirt. Ensure the soil is not too damp as wisteria is very susceptible to root rot.

To keep pests at bay, remove any leaves which are affected by cankers or spotted with mildew. The only other pest which is a concern is the wisteria borer which is present in the tissues of the vine and can lead to death. There is little that can be done if this pest attacks the wisteria bonsai.

Broadleaf Evergreen Bonsais

Adenium Bonsai

This bonsai also known as the Desert rose is native to Arabia and Africa. When in the ideal sunny location, it will yield large red, white or pink flowers. It is not as popular as an ornamental bonsai, but it easily can be made into a spectacular design. It also thrives well when in a container.

This fast growing bonsai will drop its leaves in the winter time except when located in tropical climates. As an important note, the sap of this bonsai is poisonous and needs to be handled with care and set away from animals that may disturb this plant.

The Desert Rose can be placed outside during the sunny months of May through September in the full sun or part shade. However, it must be moved into a shelter or protected when the temperatures dip below 40° Fahrenheit (5° Celsius).

Azalea Bonsai

There are approximately 1,000 subtypes of the Rhododendron family of which the commons types are Kurume azalea (Rhododendron kiusianum) and Satsuki azalea (Rhododendron indicum). They are known for their clusters of flowers which bloom during May and June with a myriad of colors from purple, red, white and pink. The leaves are dark green and range from small to medium sized.

The azaleas enjoy the sunshine but would need to be in part shade during the afternoon hours. They need to be protected from the rain to make the delicate flowers to last longer. This plant is hardy down to temperatures of 41° Fahrenheit (-5° Celsius). These bonsais must be kept in moist soil which does not have standing water. Thriving in slightly acidic soil, the azaleas should not be watered with hard water from the tap. The most appropriate is a combination of filtered tap water and rainwater.

Bird Plum Bonsai

The Sageretia theezans is also known by the name of sweet plum. It is an evergreen subtropical shrub which originally comes from Japan and China. It grows to the height of 6–9 feet (2–3 meters) and blooms in the late summer with light yellow flowers. The foliage is small and shiny light green in color and the plant produces small fruits which are blue.

The bark of the trunk is patched with dark and light brown which is similar to a sycamore tree. This is a popular choice for an indoor bonsai and is quite popular in South Asia. The bird plum required warm temperatures throughout the year and cannot withstand frost. This is a common shrub for beginners with a twist of a challenge with watering the plant sufficiently.

This plant is versatile as it can be solely an indoor plant or an outdoor plant during the summer months. It requires a place which is partly shaded when outdoors and while indoors, a window facing south or west will be ideal. This bonsai should never be placed directly in the hot sunlight.

Bougainvillea

This evergreen shrub has tiny flowers shaped like trumpets which grow in clusters which bloom from summer to fall time. The bracts of the flowers are a range of colors from purple, magenta, white, yellow, orange, pink and red. It is native to South America and is suited to most styles of bonsai. It has oval leaves that alternate on the branch.

The color of the bark is grey-beige which gets gnarly and furrowed as the bonsai matures. Since they are subtropical plants, they are not able to withstand frost and need temperatures between 50 - 59° Fahrenheit (10 - 15° Celsius) during the winter months. This bonsai is forgiving to being pruned and grow rather quickly.

For this bonsai to create magnificent flowers, it needs to receive full sun and hot temperatures during the growing season, like its native land. It is best to place the bonsai outside during the summer and then placed inside starting in the fall. It needs to stay cool and have sufficient light either by the sun or grow light.

Chinese Elm Bonsai

The Ulmus parvifolia is found commonly in China and the southeast of Asia. It can reach heights upwards to 80 feet (25 meters) and can have a thick trunk of 3 feet (1 meter) in circumference. This bonsai is easily confused with the Zelkova or Japanese Elm. An inspection of the leaves will show that the Chinese Elm has leaves that have double sets of teeth compared to the single set of teeth on the Japanese Elm. This tree grows well in part shade or full sunshine. It can ensure some frost, but it depends on which region the tree was imported. The more frost hardy varieties are from the northern parts of China. It depends on the temperature during the winter, but it is possible this bonsai will lose its leaves.

Crepe Myrtle Bonsai

The Crepe Myrtle, also known as the Lagerstroemia indica, is a deciduous tree which is subtropical. It produces flowers which are purple, white or pink and have beige bark which peels off in large sections. It is originally from Australia and South Asia.

The foliage is small and oval and they turn colors to red, orange and yellow before falling off in the fall. This bonsai can withstand a small amount of frost, but it is best to protect it from such extreme weather.

When the crepe myrtle bonsai is located in the full sun, it prevents insect and pest attacks as well as inspires the tree to flower. In addition to the sunshine, it thrives in humid climates. If located in a warm climate, this bonsai can easily be grown outdoors throughout the year. However, if located in a

28

temperate climate, it should be moved indoors to a cool place which is free of frost.

Fukien Tea Bonsai

This native of China has spread to be also found in Australia, Taiwan, Indonesia, and Japan. It is a popular bonsai plant for Western countries and still is found commonly in China. Another name the Fukien Tea Bonsai is commonly known as is the Carmona retusa.

The leaves are shiny and dark green with a small white dot on the top while fine hairs cover the underside. Petite white flowers are present during the whole year and on occasion, they create yellow-red or dark berries.

If the caregiver is located in a tropical climate, the Fukien Tea Bonsai can be cultivated outdoors all year round. Otherwise, it is a difficult bonsai tree to cultivate indoors as it requires ample amounts of sunlight as well as high humidity which is a challenge to replicate indoors. It thrives in an environment that is above 68° Fahrenheit (20° Celsius) and cannot be subject to any frigid air or frost.

Because of its tropical nature, the Fukien Tea Bonsai needs to have moist soil throughout the year. However, as always, make sure to pay special attention that the soil is not too saturated where there is standing water in the container.

Be careful with the fertilizers that are used with this variety of bonsai as the roots are quite sensitive. It is recommended to use an organic compound which is able to retain moisture yet still drains well. Use caution with the dosage when using liquid fertilizers and apply only to wet soil. A combination of pumice, Akadama and a small amount of humus is a perfect blend of soil for this bonsai tree.

The Fukien Tea Bonsai requires transplanting every two years and should be done in the early spring months. Prune as little as necessary from the root system, removing only dead sections with care.

When in unfavorable environmental conditions, the Fukien Tea Bonsai will probably suffer from infestations from whiteflies, scale, and spider mites. If this occurs, proper humidity and light need to be given to improve the tree's environment. It is also possible for this variety of bonsai to have fungal diseases attack the tree through wounds which can lead to either the branch dying or the entire plant altogether. To prevent this possibility, use the cut paste on all cuttings and wounds.

Gardenia Bonsai

The Gardenia jasminoides is an evergreen shrub which is subtropical and native to South Africa and tropical areas of Asia. It has large white flowers which are pungent along with large dark green leaves. If pollinated, the gardenia will produce orange fruits. This plant can be a challenge for the absolute beginner as it is sensitive and can be difficult to learn the ways to keep it thriving and healthy.

This bonsai is not able to withstand frost and is delicate to the idea of being moved or touched. If a spot could be found for this bonsai to be able to stay all year long, this would be the ideal situation. If you do end up moving the gardenia too much, it will stress out the tree and the buds may fall off. When the bonsai starts to flower, do not touch the petals as they will brown quickly.

The gardenia bonsai enjoys an airy and warm place which does not have direct sunlight. It thrives in temperatures between 60 - 75° Fahrenheit (16 - 23° Celsius) and no colder than 59° Fahrenheit (15° Celsius) during the winter time. Great care needs to be given to make sure the gardenia is not subjected to cold drafts as they are extremely sensitive, more so than other varieties.

Ginkgo Bonsai

The Ginkgo biloba is the oldest trees found in China as they are at least 270 million years old. Because of this fact, they are seen as a living fossil. They have fan-shaped foliage and can reach as high as 120 feet (40 meters) in natural settings. On the rare occasion, they bear fruit which has a pungent smell which is not pleasant.

The green leaves turn a vibrant yellow during the fall and then they fall off the tree. They are very hardy and able to deal with a diverse environment and soils. It is even able to deal with polluted environments and is planted along congested roadways for this reason.

This bonsai will thrive outdoors in a sunny location for the more mature trees. The juveniles are best in part shade. They are able to endure frost well when planted in the ground but should be moved to shelter or protected if in a container.

Jacaranda Bonsai

This native of South America known as Jacaranda mimosifolia has been naturalized in Australia, South Africa, the Mediterranean and the South of the United States. It grows rather large at 45 feet (15 meters) tall and 36 feet (12 meters) wide. This is a popular choice for an ornamental bonsai as it has long lived purple or blue flowers in clusters which appear during the spring and early summer and last up to eight weeks.

It has compound fern foliage along with woods seed pods which encloses the winged seeds. The bark of the tree is quite thin and grey-brown. As the tree matures, the bark starts to become scaly. The twigs of this bonsai are thin and zigzag slightly. The leaves may drop during the winter time depending on the climate and the amount of light. Most times the foliage will fall before the flowers bloom.

The Jacaranda bonsai needs an ample amount of light. It will thrive as long as it stays about the temperature of 59° Fahrenheit (15° Celsius). Keep the bonsai away from heating devices and vents.

Jade Bonsai

The Crassula is a woody shrub which grows to a height of 9 feet (3 meters). The common subtypes are Jade (Crassula ovata) and Dwarf Jade

36

(Portulacaria afra). They have a thick truck with thin branches that hold green foliage that is thick and green. If the bonsai has gone through droughts during the growing season, tiny white flowers will bloom. The juvenile bark is soft and green and changes colors to red-brown when the tree matures.

The Jade bonsai can be grown either indoors or outdoors. As long as the temperatures are high enough during the entire year, it can stay in the outside garden. This bonsai requires staying above the temperature of 41° Fahrenheit (5° Celsius). It thrives well in full sunlight.

Japanese Cherry Bonsai

With the Prunus serrulata, there began a tradition in Japan during the 8th century called Sakura. This involved appreciating and watching the development of the cherry blossom. Since this time, it has become an obsession found throughout Japan. Because of this, this is a popular choice for bonsai today in Japan.

This bonsai requires a space which is free from hard breezes and plenty of sunshine. With this said, it also needs to have a minimum of three months where the plant is cooler. It will need to be brought indoors, but it needs to continue to stay cool so it can go into dormancy. Be sure to transfer to a new container every two years. The flowers should appear in March or April depending on the location's climate.

Japanese Winterberry Bonsai

The Ilex Serrata is a small tree or shrub which only grows about 12 feet (4 meters) high. It comes originally from Japan and has a combination of dark green leaves and petite pale pink blooms. The female plants produce bright red berries which last through the winter until spring.

This outdoor tree should be in a very sunny position but out of the intense heat. If the fruits are desired, both a female and male tree need to be planted close to each other in the same type of conditions so that the flower at the same time, causing pollination.

If the berries are important, the trees need to be protected from the birds coming to eat them after they turn red. Perhaps consider some sort of cage to protect the berries if the visual of bare branches with the red berries is desired to be seen during the fall and winter months. This tree is able to tolerate frost but needs to be moved to shelter if located in a container.

Money Tree Bonsai

The Pachira aquatic is an indoor plant which is popular with the bonsai artists as it usually has a braided trunk. It is a tropical plant and a native of Central America. The name Money Tree is related to the concept of Feng Shui and is seen as a good luck tree.

This bonsai needs to be placed in a very sunny spot which will usually be a south-facing window. It can be set outside during the summer in a temperate climate in the full sun.

Olive Bonsai

The Olea europaea is native to the Mediterranean area as it has important symbolic importance. The most common subtype is the wild olive (Olea europea silvestris). This bonsai is known for having petite leaves combined with the coveted jin and shari bark. This type of bark displays the signs of survival and high age with the tree going through hostile conditions in the wild. This is an excellent beginner bonsai tree.

This is an outdoor tree that needs to be in a sunny area. This will aid the leaves in staying their signature miniature size. During the winter months, protection needs to be placed over the tree during and after the frost.

Privet Bonsai

This variety also known as Ligustrum is a hedging bonsai and is an excellent evergreen choice for beginners. There are less than 50 subtypes of the Privet. The most popular types are Vulgare (common privet), Lucidum, Japonicum, Sinense (Sinensus) and Ovalifolium (oval leaves).

These varieties are extremely strong and have thick trunks. They also follow the regular maintenance and cultivation guidelines for basic bonsai care. These benefits aid the beginner in developing solid bonsai skills.

The Privet tree thrives in an environment where there is partial direct sunlight and can be grown indoors or outdoors. When the temperature goes lower than 14° Fahrenheit (-10° Celsius) the Privet needs protection from the elements.

Broadleaf Evergreen Bonsais

Boxwood Bonsai

The Buxus sempervirens has traditionally been topiaries and hedges and are known for the strong properties which allow them to grow even in barren ground. There are over 70 subtypes with the Chinese boxwood (Buxus harlandii) and the European common boxwood (Buxus sempervirens) being the most popular for bonsai styling.

They usually have twisted branches and trunks and are a favorite with the bees who are attracted to the green-yellow flowers. They are able to be trimmed back heavily and still bud from old wood.

This bonsai can thrive in shade or full sunshine, but it is not hardy against the frost. During the winter months, it needs to be moved to a cool area such as a greenhouse with plenty of light. The winter temperatures should be around 50° Fahrenheit (10° Celsius).

Brazilian Rain Tree Bonsai

The Pithecellobium is native to the rainforests of Brazil and has lovely smelling puffy flowers which are light pink or white. The light green foliage is unique in that they have petite leaves which fold up during the evening time.

This bonsai can be kept in a container outdoors during the warm summer months as long as the sunlight is not too intense. It needs a decent amount of light and humidity. This plant does not survive from frosts or temperatures lower than 45° Fahrenheit (7° Celsius).

Brush Cherry Bonsai

The Eugenia Myrtifolia a hedge shrub which originally is from New Zealand and Australia. It bears dark green leaves and tiny white flowers during the spring. In the autumn, there are red fruits which are edible by the birds and humans alike.

This bonsai enjoys warm and sunny places. If the sun is too hot, it is best to keep it in part shade. This plant does not endure the frost and must be moved indoors or into a greenhouse during the winter. It is very picky about sudden changes in temperature. Do not use a heating device underneath the container as the roots will dry out.

Citrus Bonsai

The Citrus bonsai comes from China and develops white flowers which are fragrant. It then produces orange or yellow fruits. In respect to bonsai, the fruits and leaves are kept small. It has been naturalized throughout the world in warm climates. They are a subtropical tree with shiny dark green leaves. There are some subtypes which have thorns.

This tree thrives in the sun and heat. If the location is in a warm climate, this bonsai can be kept outdoors all year long. Other locations should place the bonsai in full sun from the months of May to September. After that time, the plant needs to be moved to a shelter such as a greenhouse, especially before the temperatures get lower than 50° Fahrenheit (10° Celsius). It should not be allowed to go dormant during the winter by storing in a warm area, with additional artificial lights to help it to survive.

Hawaiian Umbrella Bonsai

The Schefflera also goes by the name of Dwarf Umbrella Tree. It is a tropical tree native to Australia and has been naturalized in southeast Asia. It has a thin trunk and aerial roots which adds to the display. This bonsai is known for the unique pairing of compound leaves and it is not a hardwood variety as it does not produce rough bark on the branches or trunk.

It is able to be in low humidity locations along with dim light which makes it ideal for an indoor bonsai. If small leaves are desired, make sure that it gets ample light. Ideal temperatures are 65 - 72° Fahrenheit (18 - 22° Celsius) and need to be sheltered from temperatures lower than 50° Fahrenheit (10° Celsius). Keep this bonsai away cold drafts.

Japanese Holly Bonsai

This small shrub is known as Ilex Crenata and has tiny leaves, small white flowers and produced black fruits. This bonsai is native to Taiwan, Korea, Japan, and East China. It is suited to be a thick hedge and can be a mistake for Boxwood bonsai (Buxus sempervirens). For the fruits to form, there needs to be a female and male tree close to each other so they flower at the same time. This is a popular choice for bonsai gardeners.

47

This bonsai is usually sold solely as an indoor plant, but it thrives better outdoors. If in a container, it needs to be moved into a sheltered and cool place before the first frost. When the bonsai is planted into the ground, it is protected from the frost.

Myrtle Bonsai

The shrub known as Myrtus communis is from the Mediterranean and North Africa. It has dark green foliage couples with tiny white flowers which bloom during the later summer months. They are then replaced by dark blue edible fruits which contain upwards to thirty seeds each. The bark is light brown cinnamon colored. The most common type of bonsai style for this variety is the broom-style.

This bonsai requires a long and warm summer to produce the flowers. It needs to have a decent amount of airflow, especially when located indoors. If it is a hot summer, place this plant in part shade. During the fall, place the bonsai inside at a temperature about 50° Fahrenheit (10° Celsius) and it should still receive light either from grow lamps or a south-facing window. This bonsai does not tolerate frost.

Conifers & Pine Bonsai

Bald Cypress Bonsai

The Taxodium distichum is a tall tree which native to Guatemala, Mexico and the south of the United States. They grow naturally to the height of 105 feet (35 meters) and has needle foliage which drops from the tree along with thin twigs during the fall months.

It has bark that is brownish-red during the juvenile stage and then changes to a grey-brown when the tree is mature. Often there are "knees" which are wooden protrusions from the root system that appear above ground around the trunk of the tree. These can be quite large upwards to 3 feet (1 meter).

Pine Bonsais

Pines are considered popular for typical bonsai trees. The Pinus has needles that are in bundles of two or five. They naturally grow in many different shapes. It is imperative to know if it only has one or two growth spurts during the growing season to prune the tips of the branches known as candles accordingly.

For the trees which only have one growth spurt, the candles cannot be fully removed or it will cause irreversible damage. However, they can be trimmed back to make them shorter. The ones that have two growth spurts can have the first set of candles removed to encourage the second growth to produce smaller needles and candles.

The varieties of Pine bonsais that have two growth spurts are from the shores of Japan such as the Japanese Black Pine (Pinus thunbergii) and the Japanese Red Pine (Pinus densiflora).

There are many types of single growth spurt varieties such as the Japanese White Pine (Pinus parviflora), Dwarf White Pine (Myojo, Kokonoe, and Zuisho), Scots Pine (Pinus sylvestris), Ponderosa Pine (Pinus ponderosa), Mountain Pine (Pinus mugo) and the Bristlecone Pine (Pinus aristata).

Redwood Bonsai

The famous Sequoia trees which are native to northern coastal regions of California and Oregon are very tall and wide upright trees which have soft needles for foliage.

Dawn Redwoods were thought to be extinct and were made into popular choices for bonsai since 1941. They have light green needled foliage which falls off during the autumn months and has red-brown flaky bark.

The Coast Redwood is the tallest tree in the world at more than 300 feet (100 meters) while the trunk can be as thick as 21 feet (7 meters). It also has needle foliage and round cones which are small.

These bonsai would be suited for outdoors and for larger displays as they possess strong growth patterns that are a challenge to control in small bonsais.

Spruce Bonsai

This spruce coniferous tree known as Picea is found commonly throughout the northern hemisphere. They can grow to a height of 180 feet (60 meters) tall in the wild. The common bonsai subtypes are the European spruce (Picea abies), and two different types of Japanese spruce (Picea glehnii & Picea jezoensis).

They are difficult to style as the branches frequently go back to the original position after being wired and they rarely bud after being heavily pruned.

The branches are convoluted and twisted. The needle-like leaves have four sides with each side being attached directly to the branches. The leaves are on the tree anywhere from four years to a decade and the cones hang down towards the ground. The branches are bent toward the ground but the tips are pointing upwards slightly.

During the growing season, this bonsai needs to be in the full sun and moved to the part shade during the wintertime. It is recommended to protect this plant from the front when in a container. Otherwise, the roots will freeze up and kill the bonsai.

Chapter Summary

In this chapter, we covered

- A brief overview of several types of beginner and intermediate bonsai options divided by deciduous, evergreen, pine and conifers.
- The needs and environment required for these varieties of bonsai trees along with the basic anatomy.
- How to use this guide to choose the type of bonsai that you would like based on the space that you have
- In the next chapter, you will learn about the options about acquiring your new bonsai. There are several helpful tips that you need to know before you purchase online or at your local gardening store.

CHAPTER THREE

SELECTING YOUR BONSAI

The first decision you need to make is are you going to keep your bonsai: indoors or outdoors. This will determine the types of bonsais which will be available to choose from. Indoor bonsais are subtropical as they can survive indoors without direct sunlight.

Outdoor Bonsais

If you have a balcony or outdoor garden that you have a perfect spot for your new bonsai, you need to know how the basics about outdoor bonsai tree care. First off, you need to know which variation will work best for your situation. The local climate is utmost as this will determine which type will be able to withstand the temperatures. If the area you live is a Mediterranean or subtropical climate, the choices are endless; however, the sunshine and intense heat will need to be considered.

For temperate climates, the Mediterranean and subtropical trees are good choices as long as they can be placed in a greenhouse to protect from frost during the winter months. Well-draining soil will be a requirement for those living in maritime climates as the summers are rainy. However, the types of bonsai that need more full sunlight hours will not thrive well. The only choices for the continental climate bonsai owners will be the very hardy trees which are native to the area unless there is an option for protection again the frost during the winter and if part shade can be offered during the summer months.

When you have picked out the area for your new bonsai, observe the amount of sunshine the area gets during the daytime and take note of the temperatures. What are the surroundings like? Is there a lot of concrete that is going to enclose the area too much and restrict air flow? If this is the case, you will need to have shade nets for sensitive varieties. Is it an area that is in the middle of the garden with grass? This is more ideal as the humidity will be higher which will let you choose from most types of outdoor bonsai.

If the area has winds most of the time, the threat of fungal diseases and pests will be lower. However, bonsai will need more water.

If the area is shady or facing east or north, the only options that will survive are the false cypress or yew bonsai. Even so, they will not do very well without amble sunshine, so they may have more problems. If the area can be altered to allow more sunlight, this would be more ideal or consider having an indoor bonsai.

Another choice is whether you want your bonsai to have fruit or blooms? If so, check on the specific needs of the trees you want and choose which will work with space. If the tree will not acclimate well to space or the environment, it will not thrive, and owning your bonsai will be more of frustrating experiences.

It is best to have the outdoor bonsai stay potted as they will need to be moved during the winter months to stay out of the frost and trees from temperate climates will need to go into a dominancy period as well during the winter. Because they will be in pots, they will have limited space for water and nutrients.

There are specific needs of outdoor bonsai compared to indoor care. First is the light required is a minimum of three hours. If it is a conifer variety, it will need to put into full sunshine as long as possible.

If the balcony or garden does not have good airflow, this will cause low humidity. To solve this problem, you will need to place the potted bonsai on top of a tray full of water while misting the tree three times during the day.

Also, if you use a water hose to wet the walls and concrete around the tree, this will build up the humidity in the area.

It is important to check your tree throughout the day to see how dry the soil is. Because of the fluctuation in the weather, the tree may need water more and less. Watering on a schedule is not entirely possible with the outdoor plants.

The outdoor bonsai are hardy as they can withstand the cold and high temperatures given the right protection. As with any plants, they need to be protected from the winter frost, especially when the new shoots and leaves come in the early spring.

The best option for beginners is to start indoors. The temperature is able to be more controlled and the easiest and most common Ficus bonsai is an indoor tree. This is because it can thrive in the low humidity and handle a decent amount of learning curves as the beginner starts out with their first tree.

Indoor Bonsais

Caring for your indoor bonsai is different from the outdoor bonsai. First off, the lighting is going to be tricky for some owners. As stated, the tree will need to be placed in a sunny window. However, this may not be enough sunlight for the light-dependent subtropical trees. Sometimes, artificial lights will need to be used to help the bonsai to thrive. The best set up is with a fluorescent light for 10 hours each day.

High humidity is needed for most indoor bonsai varieties. This can be a tricky endeavor, but there are some methods that will help. If you place your plant on a tray filled with water, the tree will soak up the water from the base of the container. The other option is to use a mister to water your tree throughout the day. After watering time, open the window to help with airflow which will increase the humidity around the plant.

Water your plant as the soil requires and do not ever follow the directions for watering on the plant. The trees should be content with the temperatures that are set within the house throughout the year.

The temperature for indoor plants generally range between 50 - 70° Fahrenheit (10 - 21° Celsius), but you need to mimic the climate of the original location of the plant for it to fully thrive.

The bonsais should be moved from the window sill or away from cold drafts during the winter time. It is recommended to place them near a heat source so that the roots do not become too cold and start losing moisture. It will also aid in keeping the humidity levels at their prime.

Indoor tropical bonsai prefer to be in warm temperatures between 64–75° Fahrenheit (17 - 23° Celsius) during the daytime hours and then lowered slightly between 57 - 61° Fahrenheit (13 - 16° Celsius) during the evening hours. These temperatures will suffice throughout the year for the tropical variations. Indoor Mediterranean and subtropical plants are able to withstand colder temperatures, but they will thrive within these temperatures as well.

During the summer months, the tropical bonsais need to be placed in warmer areas of the home that are not too hot as they are sensitive. Temperate bonsais require an area with part or full shade. This is where it is helpful to know the variation of your bonsai to know the requirements for your tree.

Otherwise, you will notice your bonsai informing you of their stress when they are not in the ideal location.

Even though it is easier to control the temperature for the indoor bonsais, there are still threats of fluctuations in temperature. These temperature drops can occur due to windows, breezy hallways, exhaust fans, and heating systems. Be sure to place your bonsai away from these areas so that the tree will not suffer as bonsais are very sensitive to sudden temperature changes.

How to Select your Bonsai

No matter where you decide to purchase, there are basic guidelines to follow to purchase the best bonsai:

1. Purchase a tree that is suitable for the space you will be placing the bonsai.
2. Look at the tapering and shape of the trunk along with the Nebari, the above ground roots. These aspects are going to stay constant throughout the life of the tree. The branches and shoots can always be manipulated by wiring and pruning.
3. For beginners, it is best to stay with a bonsai that is easy to care for until bonsai skills are strengthened. You can always purchase a second tree at a later time.
4. Know the details of the bonsai variety that you purchase.
5. Do not buy a plant that already looks ill, malnourished or otherwise unhealthy.

The next choice is going to be if you are going to get a pre-wired and formed tree or one that you have creative license to shape the way you wish. The ready-made trees are available easily by purchasing online. There are a variety of types as well as shapes and sizes. It really comes down to how much your budget will allow.

Options for Acquiring your Bonsai

Purchasing Locally or Online

Cheap bonsais can be found at most of the garden centers, but they are not always of the best quality. Sometimes there are diamonds in the rough if you look closely. There are online stores which specialize in bonsais. They are going to be a little more expensive, but they will be of better quality.

Family owned nurseries are best to find rough bonsai trees. There are also options online to purchase a nursery stock tree, but they are higher in place rather than going in person. You will have the most luck in finding an appropriate tree from early spring through the end of summer. However, the nurseries will have stock throughout the year.

This will give you the option to see the trees first hand to see how you would like to shape and mold them. You can purchase a rough version which will require you to bend, wire and secure the branches to come to the end result you desire or look for a bonsai that is already been worked with which will require less initial maintenance.

After you have chosen your bonsai, keep the soil slightly wet. You can fertilize the tree as needed if it is purchased during the growing season. If you purchase during the early spring, the transplanting and pruning process can begin right away. If the tree is purchased at another other time during the year, wait until the spring to conduct these processes.

Directly from Nature

If you want to save money, another option is to search for a tree in the wild in your community. This option is trickier than you would possibly need permission to take the seedling or juvenile from its environment. Choose this option if you want to grow outdoors and want a native tree.

Carefully remove the tree and ensure that the entire root system is intact. Have an airy basket or container to carry the tree and transfer to a container within a couple of hours if possible to reduce the risk of shock.

The Japanese name of Sashiki is the art of taking a cutting from mature trees. This is a very common practice among seasoned bonsai gardeners and is a way that does not cost much if any money. It is also popular because it diminishes the amount of time to be able to be shaped by one year compared to growing by seed.

The best trees that are used for this process are conifers and deciduous trees. A branch from the mature tree needs to be removed that is the size of approximately 2–4 inches (5–10 cm) and no thicker than 5 mm. This is the ideal size for cutting. This should be done sure the spring and summer months.

One of the advantages of growing a bonsai from a cutting is that you can style the bonsai without the need for cutting thick branches.

The process to start plant cutting is to place a layer of the substrate such as grit or lava rock which is coarse and drains well. The next layer is going to be bonsai soil. Slice the cutting from the tree of your choice at a 45° angle using appropriate twig shears. Position the cutting into the prepared soil. If you are planting more than one, each needs to be 1 inch (2 cm) apart from each other. Water the cuttings well and keep the soil moist. You will notice the cuttings will start to grow within three weeks.

When growing your bonsai from seeds, this term is known as Misho in Japanese. Even though this process takes the longest time, it gives the owner complete control over the entire life of their bonsai. When this method is chosen, know that it will be approximately three years before the tree will be ready to start shaping and pruning.

Seeds can be gathered in many ways including purchasing online, at a local garden store or even from your own garden and community. The seeds you are acquiring are not any special variety as there are no so-called bonsai tree seeds specifically as they are simply trees from nature.

The easiest time to sow the seeds is during the fall time. However, if you want to get started any other time of the year, the variety of tree is not native to your area or the seeds were purchased online, you will need to put the seeds through a process known as stratification.

The process of stratification is where you coax the seeds to germinate even when they are not going through the cold season of winter first. Some seeds will not germinate until going through this precursory cold spell and you may need to set the seeds into the refrigerator after being soaked in water to mimic this stage. Leave the seeds in the cold up to two months before sowing into a prepared container. As this process may be challenging for a beginner, it is recommended to collect the seeds naturally and plant them in the fall.

What Container to Use?

When choosing a container, they are usually works of art within themselves. They can be simple and functional or can be elaborate and intricate masterpieces. Traditional bonsai containers are created in Japan and China and are usually earthenware which has been curled in the fire. The purpose of these pots is not only for complimenting the tree, but this type of material will not absorb moisture which allows for the tree to be able to soak up the water instead. With that said, there are plenty of conventional containers that can be used that are plastic, concrete or ceramic.

Overall, the container needs to be functional in the way that it has the proper drainage as well as sections to be able to attach wires when securing and shaping the branches. For the most part, these pots are long and shallow which aids in forming the strong root system to support this miniature tree. Only when a bonsai gardener has chosen a cascading tree, will they need to use a narrow and tall container which will serve as the center of gravity required for the root system to support this type of style.

It can prove to be a difficult task for some bonsai gardeners who are looking for the perfect complement to their overall masterpiece. Many see the container as a frame that holds art itself. Even though it is an important aspect, it must not take away from the charm or visual of the bonsai tree. Others may simply search for a functional pot until they are able to acquire and transfer the tree when the spring comes.

When choosing a container for the bonsai, there are some important aspects to consider. First, determine if your bonsai is feminine or masculine. Sometimes trees are scientifically both genders. However, the rule of thumb is if the trunk has smooth bark and curvy branches which a sparse, this is a feminine bonsai. Conversely, any tree that has deadwood, visual strength and a dense set of branches is considered masculine.

Once the gender has been chosen, this will narrow down the choices. The feminine pots usually are low and have subtle feet. They will have soft lines to accent the curves of the branches. Usually, masculine containers will have distinct feet and clean lines. If you are going for an androgynous, use a drum or round container.

The glaze that is present on the container is an important aspect of your choice. The basic color of the pot should complement a color which is present in the tree be it the flowers, fruit, leaves or the bark. Popular color choices are earth tones, gray and brown. However, this up to the individual bonsai gardener.

To find the right size pot for your bonsai, measure the tree from the top of the Nebari to the top of the tree. Then consider if the pot you want to use square, round, rectangular or oval. If you have chosen square or round, you need a pot that is 1/3 the measurement. This is going to be the depth and width of the container. If using a rectangular or oval container, then the depth will be 2/3 of the measurement.

The exception to the rule is when the foliage creates a canopy which is rather large. In this case, the width of the container is going to visually create a frame for the branches and foliage. Then the depth of the pot will decrease by the change in width to ensure the pot contains the same amount of soil. Also, trees that have flowers, fruit and grow quickly will need a deeper pot to compensate for the number of roots and the water they require.

No matter what pot you end up choosing, the goal to find the perfect container is to create a balance and harmony. Once this is accomplished, and you decided between the other details, you will be happily creating your masterpiece from the ground up.

Classification of Size

When you are purchasing a bonsai, you may see these classifications for the sizing. This is an interesting talking point between bonsai gardeners. The number of hands that are needed to move a bonsai is how they are categorized.

Keshitsubo: 1–3 inches (3–8 cm), fingertip bonsai

Shite: 2–4 inches (5 – 10 cm), fingertip bonsai

Mame: 2–6 inches (5–15 cm), fingertip bonsai

Shonin: 5 – 8 inches (13 – 20 cm), one-handed bonsai

Komono: 6 – 10 inches (15 – 25 cm) one-handed bonsai

Katade-mochi: 10 – 18 inches (25 – 46 cm), one-handed bonsai

Chui / Chumono: 16 – 36 inches (41 – 91 cm), two-handed bonsai

Dai / Omono: 30 – 48 inches (75 – 122 cm), four-handed bonsai

Hachi-uye: 40 – 60 inches (102 – 152 cm), six-handed bonsai

Imperial: 60 – 80 inches (152 – 203 cm), eight-handed bonsai

Chapter Summary

In this chapter, we covered

- What to look for when purchasing a bonsai plant.
- Where to purchase or acquire a tree, seeds or seedlings.
- How to choose the perfect container.
- In the next chapter, you will learn how to care for your new bonsai.

It will give you guidelines on the soil choices, watering your bonsai properly and choosing the correct fertilizer. There are also individual care tips for the bonsais varieties.

CHAPTER FOUR

CARE GUIDE FOR YOUR BONSAI

There are many factors such as the time of year, the climate locally and available sunlight hours in addition to whether it is going to be an indoor or outdoor bonsai.

If you are going to keep your plant indoors, it is best to find a sunny south-facing window so that the bonsai will receive as much sunlight hours as possible. It needs to be placed on the sill or as close as possible to the window as the intensity of the light is going to diminish the further you place it away from the window.

There are many bonsais that require higher humidity. There are two popular options to assist with this. First, you can simply spray water onto the plant when you are watering. The other option is to place the container onto a small tray which has water inside.

Outdoor trees can be planted into the ground or in a container. If the temperature does not allow for the tree to stay outside through the cold winter, it should be placed into a container and a winter location will need to be chosen in accordance with needs of the bonsai.

The ideal spot in the garden is going to be the sunniest area. If the climate you are located in has intense sunlight, shelter should be provided to protect the health of the tree.

Once you choose a bonsai, be sure to research the exact environmental needs it requires.

Soil Basics

There are some varieties of bonsai that require a special mix for their growth medium. Most bonsais will require soil which will drain well so that the threat of root rot is minimized. Search further in this chapter for your bonsai species and find what is needed for your tree.

You have the option to purchase premixed soil or you can save some money and combine them yourself. This option also gives you more control. Do not use regular garden soil as it becomes rather hard when it is dry which will not bode well for the root system of the bonsai. Purchase the best quality soil mixtures possible as it has a large impact on the vigor and health of your bonsai.

It is recommended to not use organic mixes, even when advertised for bonsais. These soils are mixed with bark, dead leaves or peat and will continue to break down over time. When this happens, it will reduce the drainage of the soil and possibly lead to root rot. Also, if you purchased your plant from a wholesale or garden center, it is best to re-pot as the quality of the soil is likely to be lower.

In reading through the specifics for the bonsai varieties, there may be suggestions for specific soil combinations to be made. The most common admixtures for soil are fine gravel, lava rock, pumice, and Akadama.

The gravel will aerate the soil as well as in aid in draining. This component is more old school as there are other better options. However, some plants thrive better with gravel combined in the soil. The lava rock helps the soil to retain water. Also, roots are not able to grow into the rocks.

Pumice is used because it absorbs nutrients and water very well. It is a volcanic matter which is soft. When this is combined with the soil, it helps the root system to evenly grow and extract essential nutrients of the soil.

Akadama is a specialized Bonsai soil component that is Japanese clay which has been baked. Before it is mixed with the soil, it needs to be sifted to ensure the dust is removed. Because it is a specialized product, it can be expensive and sometimes is substituted for alternative clays that are commonly available. Some bonsai gardeners also use cat litter in place of Akadama as it has the same effect.

As a general guide, the soil composition for the deciduous bonsais should be 50% Akadama, 25% lava rock, and 25% pumice. For the pine or coniferous trees, a combination of equal parts of Akadama, pumice and lava rock should be used. Refer to the guide further in this chapter to see if there is another recommendation for your bonsai.

Watering Basics

Because each plant is different for their watering needs, it is best to look at the individual tree under the care guide in chapter five to know for sure. There are some varieties who enjoy being watered quite often. Others do not require much water at all.

A general tip that works for bonsais is to water the soil when it gets dry on the surface. This will ensure that the soil is never completely dry all the way through. This will ensure that the root system is not drying out from lack of water and nutrients.

Because the needs of the bonsai differ throughout the year depending on whether it is in growing or dormant season, there is no way to be able to water these trees on a schedule. Refrain from using cold water during the afternoon hours as this shocks the tree because the soil is usually warmed from the sunshine.

As long as you follow the individual guidelines for your bonsai and you keep the soil at the moisture level that is ideal, you will have no problems with keeping your tree watered correctly.

Fertilizer Basics

Because the bonsais are in pots which are petite, they need to have the nutrients replenished regularly. This is especially important during the growing season. Naturally, the juvenile trees are going to need more fertilization as they grow and as they mature, they will need fewer nutrients. However, just like the watering, it depends on the factors of the overall health of the bonsai, the time of the year and also the variety. To see exactly what is needed for your specific species, look further in this chapter to find how frequently you need to feed your tree. This will also inform you if there is any specialized fertilizer required.

As a general rule for outdoor plants, the bonsais will need more nitrogen during the spring and then diminish through the fall months. Some bonsai gardeners will also use a more balanced fertilizer throughout the growing season. Be sure to monitor your tree for signs of malnutrition such as the leaves curling, wilting or changing colors and adjust the fertilizer for the bonsai's needs. The indoor bonsais will require feeding throughout the year and it is best to use a balanced fertilizer which is liquid.

Of course, there are variations to these rules. If you want to have the bonsai go through the flowering stages, use a fertilizer which is high in Phosphorus content if a juvenile tree. For more mature trees, lower the Nitrogen levels to encourage them to bloom.

There is a synthetic and organic version of fertilizer which comes in a solid or liquid form. This comes down to the personal preference of the bonsai gardener as there is little difference between these choices. Another way to fertilize your Bonsai shrubs and trees is to use organic pellets which slowly release the required nutrients into the soil for a longer period compared to weekly or biweekly treatments with liquid fertilizers.

If you choose to use solid fertilizer, you can utilize a cover. This will ensure that it is not washed away or possibly disturbed by birds and animals when located outside. The liquid fertilizer should be applied when watering the plant by following the instructions on the bottle.

Remember that you are feeding your bonsai when you apply the fertilizer. If you do not want to stimulate growth but level it out, you can reduce the amount or frequency that you feed the bonsai. It is important to not overfeed the trees as more is not better in this instance.

Repotting Basics

The purpose of transplanting your bonsai to a new pot is to give the tree new nutrients, so that is can continue to thrive and grow. It gives the bonsai gardener the opportunity to cut back the root system as needed to remove the old roots that are no longer serving the plant and to see the progress of the tree's development. It will also let you know if you need to adjust the water as you will be able to inspect the root system for overall health.

During the early spring, gently remove the bonsai from the container to inspect the roots. If they are compact and not much soil remains, it is time to transplant. The reason this is done in the early spring is that the bonsai is in dormancy which will shock the treeless by changing the environment. Also, if the fragile roots have been damaged during the process, they will quickly start to grow back.

Special Treatment of Certain Varieties

Adenium Bonsai

This bonsai requires little water and should be only watered every week to 10 days. Be sure not to over water this plant.

Liquid fertilizer is recommended once a week during the spring to fall months at half the recommended dose. Replanting in a new container every other year is advised during the spring. Use a soil that drains very well as this bonsai does not like any standing water or excess moisture.

If this bonsai is in a weakened state, infestations from spider mites, mealy bugs or aphids may become a problem. If all the care guides are followed, there should be no issue with these types of pests.

Azalea Bonsai

The azalea bonsai needs to be transplanted to a new container every two years. During the spring or summer immediately after the flowers have died are the best times to transfer to new soil. The root system of the azalea is tangled and fragile, so take great care in pruning back the dead or frail roots before putting into a new pot. The soil which is required for the azaleas is solely Kanuma which is free of lime.

The azalea bonsais require a specialized fertilizer for rhododendron or azaleas. They come in solid and liquid forms, with the liquid forms lasting longer periods of time between feedings. During the months of May and June when the azalea is blooming, cut the fertilizer in half.

Pests are rare with the azalea bonsai unless there is low humidity. This will create the perfect environment for spider mites. If this should happen, the entire bonsai should be treated with a specialized pesticide and then measures should be taken to correct the humidity levels.

Root rot is a common issue with azalea bonsais when they are allowed to sit in water. It is caused by a fungus and can quickly kill your azalea if not remedied. Start to only water when the soil is slightly dry and do not over water.

Another fungus which is common to azaleas is leaf galls. The results of this fungal infection are the leaves and branches become pale green and thick during the spring and summer months. The final stage of the infection is when there is a powdery white substance on the foliage and branches which then become hard and brown. This fungus is also related to too much water which even includes rainwater.

Bald Cypress Bonsai

These bonsai trees need ample warmth and full sunlight during the growing season. If located in a warm environment, it can be a year-round outdoor bonsai. If located in a container, it should be moved indoors or into a greenhouse at the first sign of frost.

During the summer growing season, this bonsai requires a substantial amount of water. For those who are not available to water so frequently, place a shallow dish under the container which is full of water. Bald Cypress is often found in swamps and lakes and can stand to be in standing water. When the leaves have fallen in the wintertime, less water will be required, but the soil should never go completely dry.

Liquid fertilizer should be used every week from spring to fall. Juvenile trees need re-potted every other year with the roots pruned back about 30%. Mature trees can get a new container every three to five years.

Bird Plum Bonsai

When the bonsai is indoors during the winter, the ideal temperature should be between 53 - 72° Fahrenheit (12 - 22° Celsius). If the higher temperatures are present, more light is going to be required which can easily be acquired through a grow light. This bird plum also thrives well in high humidity conditions.

The soil must be kept moist and not have any standing water. The main issue with the care of this plant is the lack or abundance of water. The roots are very sensitive, and it is quite possible to have the bonsai die relatively quickly when the water care is not precise. It is utmost important to check the soil a few times a day to see if it will require water as even one or two days without checking can lead to dire circumstances.

The composition of the soil that the bird plum thrives is neutral or slightly acidic so calcareous water should be avoided. To aid with the humidity levels, spray the bonsai with water free from lime. Either solid or liquid fertilizer can be used. During the growing months, apply liquid fertilizer each week and every four weeks if utilizing solid fertilizer. During the dormant months of winter, this time frame can be doubled.

During the entire year, the shoots of the bird plum can be pruned back. However, if you want the bonsai to bear flowers and fruits, do not trim during the late summer. Any wiring of the shoots and branches should be completed in the spring as they get too hard to bend as the tree matures. Once the basic structure of the branches has been acquired, the need for wiring will not be necessary.

Using a standard mix of soil which drains well, transplant the bonsai to another container every two years. Prune back the roots as much as 30% when transferring to the new pot. To aid in the water issue, a larger pot can be chosen which will diminish the chance of the bonsai not having enough water. If the leaves have turned to a pale green, use less calcareous water and add some ferric fertilizer to the soil to remedy this issue.

Common pests of whitefly or aphids can be a nuisance with the bird plum bonsai. This usually occurs due to the low amount of humidity. Treat the infestation with a specific pesticide and create more humidity in the space of the bonsai. Sometimes mildew can occur if there is not enough air circulation which can be remedied by correcting the issue and using a fungicide on the plant.

Bougainvillea

The pH of the soil that the bougainvillea prefers is between 6 and 6.5. Avoid any water with high calcareous content. This plant will require a decent amount of water when the soil becomes dry but do not waterlog the soil as it leads to insects, fungal infections, root rot, and death.

Feed this bonsai each month using solid fertilizer or every week using the liquid fertilizer during the summer months. It can extend to double the time during the dormant winter months.

Transplanting to a new pot every two to three year during the spring is ideal. For mature trees, it can be between three to five years to place in a new container. Any well-draining soil can be used with the bougainvilleas. Use caution when removing the bonsai from the pot as the root system is very delicate and will tear easily. Tenderly untangle the roots and prune back the old and dead sections before placing in the new container.

When this bonsai is able to be in ideal conditions, pests tend to stay away. The plants that are weakened by poor conditions will possibly be subject to caterpillars, whitefly, mealy bug, scale, aphids, and mildew. If any of these infestations occur, use a specific pesticide to remove them. Then get to the base of the problem that caused them to attack the tree in the first place.

Boxwood Bonsai

The boxwood needs plenty of water during the growing season of the summer. However, it can withstand short stints of drought. Do not have standing water in the soil. Tap water will be sufficient for this bonsai as it prefers to have a pH of 7 to 8.

This plant should be feed weekly with liquid fertilizer or each month with solid during the summer. Avoid feeding during the dormant winter months. The exception to this rule is the Chinese boxwood which should continue to be fertilized once a month through the winter.

When this plant is repotted every two to five years, there needs to be a combination of lime rock gravel or pumice added to the regular soil mixture. Be sure to cut back all the dead and dying roots as it can withstand having up to 30% of the roots cut back.

There are many pests and diseases that plague this bonsai. The fungal diseases of Phytophthora root rot and blight including the infestations from boxwood psyllid, boxwood leafminer, boxwood mite, scale, and nematodes are common as well. For these issues, use the specific pesticides and fungicides to eliminate the problems. If it is a serious case, a professional may need to be consulted.

Other pests include the boxwood moth which has started to become an incredible issue in Europe. Use Bacillus thuringiensis or Neem oil to remedy this infestation. Also there long green caterpillars which will eat the foliage of the bonsai very quickly. Once noticed, these can be picked off the plant by hand.

Brazilian Rain Tree Bonsai

Never let the soil dry out completely. Use a spray bottle to apply water to the foliage to assist with higher humidity levels when kept indoors.

Feed with liquid fertilizer four times during the growing season months and then only once during the winter time. A well-draining soil should be used when repotting every other year. Do not cut back more than 20% of the root system.

This tree is very resistant to infestations and diseases. Pests that attack this bonsai are nematodes which effect the root nodules which are throughout the root system. If this occurs, use a nematicide. When the plant is kept indoors, it is susceptible to infestations from white flies, spider mites and aphids. Use the specified pesticide to control the infestation. Adjust the humidity levels by spraying water on the bonsai.

Brush Cherry Bonsai

When the soil gets dry, water this shrub thoroughly. Avoid using unfiltered tap water and instead, use collected rainwater. Spray the bonsai during the water to force the humidity level up.

Feed by using an acidic fertilizer made for azaleas twice a month during the spring to fall. Only feed once a month during the winter time. Make sure to transfer this bonsai every other year during the spring. Cut back the dead roots, but do not remove more than 20%. Use Kanuma in the new container for the growth medium.

The bonsai can by bothered by spider mites, aphids, Caribbean fruit fly, mealy bugs and scale. Use the specific pesticides to eliminate these infestations.

Chinese Elm Bonsai

The Chinese Elm needs to be watered thoroughly when the soil becomes dry. Be sure to not over or under water this tree.

A fertilization compound of liquid and solid would be ideal for this bonsai. Feed the Chinese elm once a week using this method and do not feed any fertilizer during the winter if in a tormented state while being stored in a cold place.

The juvenile bonsais should be transplanted to a new container every other year during the spring. The more mature trees can wait three to four years between transplants. When they are re-potted, cut back the old and dying roots. This tasks can be challenging as the root system is intertwined and crooked. Re-pot into good draining soil.

When the humidity is low, these bonsais are prone to attacks from scale and spider mites. Treat the infestation with pesticides. Also, remedy the humidity issue by spraying the tree with water to build up the humidity level. Avoid any products with lime or sulfur as the tree will react by losing all the foliage.

Chinese Pepper Bonsai

When the soil surface becomes dry, you must water this bonsai until all the soil is watered thoroughly. However, do not let this plant stand in water. During the growing season of the summer, this shrub requires a decent amount of water. However, the amount can be cut back considerably during the wintertime. If there is a heating device near or underneath the bonsai, ensure that the roots do not dry out.

Fertilizer twice a month during the spring to fall months and cut back to once a month during the wintertime. They need to be repotted every other year and have the roots pruned back. Be sure to remove no more than 30% and take away the dying or dead roots only. Use a compound of soil which are equal parts humus, pumice, and Akadama.

On rare occasion, the scale will attack this bonsai. Be sure to use a specific pesticide to remove completely. Another pest which is a nuisance is the spider mite. These will infest the shrub during the winter months when in a shelter. Keep monitoring the bonsai even when in the dormant period.

Citrus Bonsai

During the summer, water this bonsai regularly when the soil surface is dry. It can withstand short periods of drought. The soil must drain well to keep the tree out of standing water. This bonsai will require less water during the winter. Be sure to use water free from lime.

Specialized fertilizers for citrus plants must be used each week from spring through fall. It can be diminished down to once a month during the winter. In the spring, transfer to a new pot with an acidic soil combined with peat. Perform this every other year.

The common pests for the bonsai are vine weevils, leaf-miner fly, mealy bugs, scale, and spider mites. These attacks are common when it is too warm and not enough light. Use pesticides specific to the infestation and change the location of your bonsai.

Crepe Myrtle Bonsai

During the summer growing season, the crepe myrtle soil should never go dry. If the correct amount of humidity is created, this will help the watering situation. This bonsai will require less water during the winter months when it is dormant. Fertilizer should be added every two weeks and can be solid or liquid.

The crepe myrtles need to be transplanted every two to three years. The soil needs to be a mix of 10% fertilizer, 40% regular soil and 50% organic compound.

On occasion, this bonsai is troubled by aphids. Use a water hose to remove with a strong jet of water or just an insecticide instead. A much more common issue with the crepe myrtles is mildew. Keep monitoring your bonsai to catch this problem as soon as possible. If found, use a fungicide to resolve the issue.

Ficus Bonsai

When caring for your Ficus Bonsai, it is imperative to keep your tree in temperatures above 59° Fahrenheit (15° Celsius) as they cannot withstand the frost. These Bonsai trees require many hours of full sun or artificial ultraviolet rays as possible. With this said, the temperature needs to stay rather consistent so that you do not shock the Bonsai. As a note, the humidity is not as important with the Ficus variety; however, if you are interested in getting the aerial roots, the humidity must be as close to 100% as possible. To help assist with this type of environment, daily misting of the Ficus Bonsai is required.

Because this is an easy beginner plant, this tree is more flexible with the watering procedure. You can over or under water the Ficus on occasion without any ill effects. Simply water when the dirt is becoming dry. During the winter months, more water is necessary and the soil only needs to be slightly wet.

The Ficus trees need more fertilizer during the summer months. No more than 2 weeks should go by without fertilizing your Bonsai. If your Bonsai is still growing during the winter months, the amount of time doubles to 4 weeks that it needs fertilizer.

The beauty of the Ficus Bonsai is that it is possible to fuse sections of the plant together when pressure is applied. This method can be used for the trunks, roots, and branches. As an example, several plants can be tied together so that it creates one large trunk and root system. Grafting is also a technique that fairs well with the Ficus Bonsais which gives the caregiver much more creative space to be as artistic as they please with the display.

It is suggested to transplant your Ficus Bonsai every 2 years during the springtime months. At this time, the caregiver can cut back the roots as necessary and report in a basic mixture of soil.

Gardenia Bonsai

Ideally, the gardenia bonsai would be watered with rainwater due to the plant thriving in acidic soil. Do not have the bonsai in standing water. Only keep the soil slightly wet. If it is an indoor bonsai, use a spray bottle to apply lime-free water.

This tree ideally will have liquid fertilizer every two weeks during the growing months of spring through fall. It would be cut back to once a month during the winter months.

During the spring every two to three years, the gardenia bonsai needs to be transplanted. Only cut away the dead roots and do not take more than 15% of the root mass. Use Kanuma or other acidic soil that will drain well. Consider also using a product to combat again possible chlorosis.

The gardenia bonsais are prone to attacks from mealy bugs, scale, and aphids. They will affect the roots and leaves. These insects will produce the honeydew residue which can also lead to mold. Remove the infestation with a specific insecticide.

Ginkgo Bonsai

The soil needs to be slightly moist during the winter months and needs ample water during the rest of the year. However, be sure not to over water. Begin feeding the bonsai when the buds start to open with a nitrogen-rich fertilizer during the spring.

This will encourage new shoots to grow and this will improve the foliage overall. Feed the tree once a week until the fall time when the leaves start to turn yellow.

During the spring, transfer the juvenile trees every year. Once the bonsai matures, it can be every two to five years before needing a new container. Use well-draining soil and do not cut back the roots too much.

Pests, diseases and fungal infections are extremely rare for this bonsai as it is used to being in less than ideal conditions.

Hawaiian Umbrella Bonsai

The soil must not dry out for this bonsai as it takes an ample amount of water during the growing season. Be more careful about over water during the winter time and do not place over a heating source.

Liquid fertilizer should be used on a weekly basis from the spring through the fall. It needs to be only once a month during the winter months. Use standard soil to transfer the bonsai to another container. Be extra careful with the brittle roots and only remove what is necessary. This needs to be done during the spring every other year.

This tree is rarely infested with pests. However, the scale can be a nuisance and in that case, use an oil-based pesticide to remove the problem.

Jacaranda Bonsai

The soil of the Jacaranda needs to remain slightly wet. If the plant is not receiving enough water, the leaves will shrivel, turn brown and fall off the tree. In the case of over-watering, the leaves will turn yellow and fall off the bonsai.

Liquid fertilizer is recommended for this bonsai. It should be applied once a week during the growing season and twice a month during the winter months.

Major pruning should be conducted in the spring when the largest leaves will be removed to prepare for the growing season. When at least 5 leaf pairs have grown, cut back the shoots to only one or two pairs of leaves.

Wiring is a possibility as long as they are removed within three months so that damage is not made on the branches. Only use wire on the juvenile branches as they will be more flexible.

Every two years during the spring is when the Jacaranda needs to be transplanted to a new pot. The soil needs to drain well.

The scale is a concern as it periodically attacks this bonsai. Use an insecticide which contains oil to eliminate the threat.

Jade Bonsai

Because the leaves are so thick, they hold a large amount of water. Due to this, only water this bonsai about once a week during the growing season. When the plant is cold during the winter time, it can go as long as three weeks before watering. Monitor the soil and water when it gets slightly dry. The beauty about this bonsai is you do not need to worry as much about overwatering and the resulting root rot.

During the growing season, this bonsai needs to be fertilized once a month. Every other year, repot the plant in the spring. Use soil which drains well, but does not water the soil for about 5 days after transplanting or you will risk root rot.

Japanese Elm

If you are located in extremely sunny conditions, it is best to place the Japanese Elm Bonsai in a semi-shaded area during the hottest summer months. Water needs careful monitoring and balance as you do not want to over water your tree, but you do not want to have the roots dry out. You also want to use water free of chalky limestone to help your tree to grow properly.

Japanese Holly Bonsai

Place the Japanese Holly in a place with an ample amount of sunshine but not too intense. If in a tropical area, plant the bonsai in the part shade. Water this plant regularly when the soil surface gets dry.

Liquid fertilizer should be given four times a month during the growing season. Transfer to a new container in the spring every other year. Use a mixture of 40% pumice, 40% Akadama and 20% humus as the grow medium. Conduct a root pruning while transferring and do not cut more than 20% of the root system.

If infestations from vine weevils, leaf-miner moths or spider mites attack the Japanese Holly, treat with a specific pesticide.

Japanese Maple

You can grow the Japanese Maple Bonsais indoors or outdoors; however, it may be slightly easier outside if you have a somewhat shady spot to position the shrub. This variety is not able to handle direct heat as the leaves will become damaged. The environment should be no less than 14° Fahrenheit (-10° Celsius) even though this plant is frost resistant.

You should set a daily watering routing for the Maple Bonsais especially during the growing season. Depending on the moisture of the soil, you may need to water your shrub several times a day if it is rather hot or in the midst of its vigorous growing stage. Make sure to apply water which is low in levels of lime and nitrogen as the Japanese Maple Bonsais thrive in neutral or slightly acidic pH levels of soil.

Organic fertilizers are ideal for the Japanese Maple Bonsais and can be coupled with weekly liquid fertilizers to result in quicker growth. The biggest precaution is to refrain from extremely high levels of nitrogen in the soil.

Japanese Winterberry Bonsai

When the soil becomes dry, be sure to water this bonsai thoroughly. It cannot dry out completely. Use either a solid or liquid fertilizer four times a month during the growing season of the spring through the fall. It needs to be put into a new container every other year with all the dead and dying roots being removed. The best combination of soil for this bonsai is 40% pumice, 40% Akadama and 20% humas.

On occasion during the springtime, aphids will infest this bonsai. They can usually be easily controlled and removed with insecticides.

Juniper Bonsai

The Juniper Bonsai varieties must be grown outdoors as it requires as much natural sunlight as possible. Protective measures must be exercised when the temperatures get below 14° Fahrenheit (-10 ° Celsius). If you notice that the leaves turn a dark purplish brown during the winter months, there is no need to worry. This is a natural reaction of the Juniper Bonsais to protect themselves against frost. During the spring, the foliage will turn green once again.

As for watering, you need to monitor the soil moisture as the roots do not fair well in over-saturated soil. Juniper Bonsais should only be watered when the soil is starting to become dry. Misting should be part of the regular routine as it grows well in humid conditions.

As a general rule, the Juniper Bonsais are very resistant to pest infestations given that they are receiving enough sunshine and have enough airflow through the foliage. Still, the caregiver will need to monitor the pest situation on a regular basis as the Junipers are subject to webworms, needle miner, aphids, scale, and mites as well as rust fungus. If the caregiver encounters any of the infestations, the cause needs to be discovered as the pests will continue to come back even with treatment.

In regards to the rust fungus, the subtypes of Junipers with the green-blue leaves will be more resistant to these infections compared to the yellow-green foliage varieties. The rust fungus will cause swollen brown sores on the leaves and will infect the tree permanently so it is important to keep monitoring the Juniper trees for signs of infection.

To counteract the fungus, a caregiver can try to remove the infected areas, but there is no guarantee this will not affect the remaining foliage. Most caregivers will burn a plant which is infected with rust fungus as it will easily transfer to other trees, causing an unending cycle.

Money Tree Bonsai

Feed this bonsai with fertilizer once a week during the growing season of spring to the middle of fall. The Money Tree needs to be transplanted to a new pot every two to three years during the spring before the buds start to grow. Use a soil which has good drainage.

Myrtle Bonsai

Avoid having standing water in the container but never let the soil dry out completely. Do not use unfiltered tap water as this plant does not respond well to lime. Rainwater is bests used to hydrate.

Liquid fertilizer is needed weekly during the growing season. If the bonsai is kept dormant during the fall and winter months, do not feed. If not in dormancy, feed every other week.

For juvenile bonsais, re-pot every other year. When they mature, you can wait from every three to five years to transfer to a new container. The ideal soil would be a mixture of regular soil with Kanuma or peat.

Common pests which invade the myrtle is whitefly, mealy bug and scale. This will occur when there is a lack of light and no air flow. Create a healthier place for your bonsai and use pesticides to rid the tree of infestation.

Olive Bonsai

This plant needs to be fertilized on a monthly basis with solid matter during the growing season of spring to the middle of fall. It needs to be transplanted every three to four years. The ideal time is in the spring before the buds begin to grow. A special mix of soil is not necessary and needs to drain well.

Pine Bonsais - Single Growth Spurt Varieties

Most of the care instructions are the same as the Pine bonsai which has two growth spurts except that the single growth trees need to be feed fertilizer throughout the year. If the tree is in ill health, refrain from feeding. Otherwise, fertilize only during the early spring through the end of fall.

Since the candles are only going to be trimmed once during the end of spring of the beginning of summer, cut them down to the instructed 5 mm. Remove the surplus shoots during the spring or the fall.

Pine Bonsai - Two Growth Spurt Varieties

The reason why these specific subtypes lose their first candles, causing a second growth spurt, is because terrible storms cause the foliage to come off the tree naturally. Because this tree has adapted over time, there is a variation in the way that spruce trees from Japan grow.

These storms generally happen in the middle of the summer. Bonsai gardeners will usually mimic these "storms" by removing the candles which are the tips of the branches. This causes the second growth spurt to occur rather quickly and lasts through the fall months. Ensure you acquire this type of pine bonsai if you have a long growing season available. This will give the second growth time to fully develop.

This bonsai needs to be outdoors in the full sunshine. This will aid in the proper timing of the growth periods and ensure that the needles do not grow long. When the trees are in containers, they will need to be protected from the winter frosts.

Do not over water this tree as it does not thrive when constantly in wet conditions. Good draining soil is a requirement as well as to have protection from large amounts of rainfall, especially during the second growth. Keeping excess moisture away from the bonsai during this time will make sure that the needles do not grow too long.

Feed the trees from March until the early summer until the candles are removed. Then use a solid fertilizer during the month prior to the removal of the candles each week. Do not feed after cutting the candles until the second set of candles have become hard. Then start feeding again until the end of fall. Transplant every year during the spring before the buds start to grow.

Pests of the Pine bonsai are caterpillars, scale, spider mites, and aphids. Use specific pesticides to eliminate the infestation and try to get more sunlight onto the tree. On rare occasions, fungal diseases will affect the tree. In this case, get an expert opinion as the pines are very likely to die once disease sets in.

Redwood Bonsai

They thrive in sunny spaces, but where the sun is too intense, it should be moved to a part shade area. When these bonsais are in a container, they will need to be placed in a shelter such as a greenhouse when the winter frost comes.

The soil needs to continue to stay moist but not have any standing water. They require an enormous amount of water during the summer while at the peak of the growing season. Use a fertilizer that is high in nitrogen in the springtime. While in the summer months, cut back the feeds substantially as the bonsai will grow too quickly otherwise.

Every other year, these trees need to be moved to another container because the root system will fill up the pot. Vigorously cut back the root system of any stray, dying or dead roots, but take care not to remove any central part of the root system. The soil does not require a specific pH, but it needs to drains well.

It is extremely rare for any pests, disease or infections to occur to the Sequoias.

Spruce Bonsai

When the soil becomes dry, thoroughly water but do not allow to stand in water. During the winter, do not let the roots completely, but water the bonsai less.

Every four weeks, solid fertilizer can be added to feed the bonsai during the growing season. If you chose liquid fertilizer, you will only need to apply it once a month during the spring through the fall time. Spruce also thrive from leaf feeding which aids the plant to continue to keep its dark green color in the foliage. If you spray liquid fertilizer with iron and chelates for the foliage.

Every other year, transplant the bonsai to another container for juvenile trees. For mature trees, it can be between four and five years before repotting. Do not prune the roots more than 15% and even less for mature trees. Use a soil mix that drains well with a mix of staple grains.

The spruce is susceptible to many fungal diseases such as needlecast or rust which will affect the foliage. Use fungicides to remove the issue. Pests such as caterpillars, spruce budworms, spruce needle miners, gall adelgids, spruce spider mites, and green spruce aphids can affect the bonsai at any time. Keep monitoring your tree and use specific pesticides as needed to control the infestation.

Wisteria Bonsai

The Wisteria bonsai requires full sunlight especially during the growing season as this results in the full flowering capabilities of the vine. If the Wisteria bonsai is grown naturally outdoors, they are very hardy against the frost. However, this is not the case if they have been transplanted into containers. In this case, keep them inside or in a greenhouse to keep them protected from the extreme winter weather.

The Wisteria bonsai require full sunlight especially during the growing season as this results in the full flowering capabilities of the vine. If the Wisteria bonsai is grown naturally outdoors, they are very hardy against the frost. However, this is not the case if they have been transplanted into containers. In this case, keep them inside or in a greenhouse to keep them protected from the extreme winter weather.

Water is extremely important during the growing season as the Wisteria bonsai use large amounts during the spring and summer months. During the fall and winter time, the watering schedule needs to be altered to ensure the soil is slightly moist.

Chapter Summary

In this chapter we covered,

- Instructions on the methods to combine soil and fertilizer compounds to ensure your bonsai will get the nutrients they need.
- A guide for watering tips which will help to keep your plant from having issues with the root system failing.
- Specific care requirements for different varieties of bonsai to include how many times to water, the timing of fertilizing and re-potting as well as pest control tips.
- In the next chapter, you will learn how to style and shape your bonsai. There is a comprehensive guide to beginner wiring techniques as well as pruning basics.

CHAPTER FIVE

STYLING & SHAPING YOUR BONSAI

Certain techniques are used when cultivating and shaping a Bonsai tree including wiring or pruning branches and pinching buds. These techniques are utilized to promote and redirect the healthy growth of the Bonsai. Even though most of the Bonsai trees are no more than four feet tall, they are not meant to be such small plants genetically.

Pruning

The purpose of pruning is to replicate the tree as it would look in nature as much as possible. The months that you need to prune are during the spring and summer. Be sure to purchase the correct tools for your bonsai as you will need different tools for a younger tree compared to a mature tree.

It is wise to have a concave cutter on thicker branches as the wounds that are created will heal much quicker than using normal cutters. The best way to know how you want to shape and prune your tree is to study designs to know what final display you are going for. Then you slowly work each year to reach that goal as your bonsai grows taller and stronger.

The best way to understand how to prune a bonsai is to know how the trees grow. Usually, trees will grow more on the top of the tree rather than the outer or lower branches. This idea is known as apical dominance which allows the tree to grow taller in a competition of sunshine from other nearby trees. Because the foliage is thicker on the top of the tree, the sunlight is not able to penetrate the inner limbs. Eventually, the leaves and branches will start to die away. This is the complete opposite which is required for the art of bonsai.

There are two types of pruning. The one that is performed the most is maintenance pruning. This is to remove any obvious flaws in the design at designated times through the growing season and sometimes throughout the year. The other type is known as structural pruning. This is where the heavy cutting occurs which will give the bonsai its simplified style or shape.

Maintenance pruning is the method to counteract apical dominance. When encountered, the remedy is to defoliate or prune specific branches to allow more sunshine as well as airflow to the middle of the tree. In turn, this encourages the tree to redistribute growth to not only the top section. This can be done throughout the year unless it says otherwise under your specific bonsai later in this chapter. This ideally should be performed from the months of March through September.

For other areas of the tree, cut twigs or shoots which have outgrown the canopy size or shape. You should use normal cutters or shears to minimize damage. Pay special attention to the top and outer sections of your bonsai.

In the case of Pine bonsais, the leaves should be pinched by hand rather than clipped with shears. Because of the frail nature of their needled foliage, pinching allows for the smallest amount of damage.

Another method of maintenance pruning is known as defoliation. This process is for the deciduous trees which in the leaves are systematically removed. This process makes the bonsai create new leaves and also results in smaller leaves being produced.

Structural pruning is usually done once a year at a designated time. This is where whole branches or structures can be removed. Be sure to look at your specific plant requirements as you keep reading. This is a difficult part of the process as the decision is irreversible and it can be challenging to think ahead to how the tree will look with and without the limb as it grows. These heavy prunings usually take place during the early spring. Sometimes it is not until the end of fall.

The best way to perform structural pruning is to move the bonsai to a table which is at eye level. Take away all the dead wood from the tree. Sit and observe your tree in detail as you evaluate the tree in front of you and the ultimate design. This will aid you in determining if any alterations need to be made. The general rule of thumb is to cut no more than 1/3 of the bonsai's foliage. There are some guidelines you may wish to follow; however, the gardener uses their design as their final blueprint.

The cuts that should be made while performing structural pruning are:

- Shoots which are growing from the base and top of the trunk

- Branches that are obscuring the trunk from being viewed

- Limbs that are hanging close to the ground

- Dead branches and leaves

- Branches which are crossing each other, unless you want to wire into a different location

- Interior branches which are not growing outwards

- Branches that are unpredictable with their twists and turns

- Two branches which are growing side by side. One should be chosen for removal

- Trim limbs which are beyond the profile or canopy of the tree

- Thick branches at the top of the tree which look disproportionate

The danger with cutting large limbs is that scarring can easily occur. This depends on the size of the wound and the location. It also matters which tools you used to remove the branch. Ideally, a concave cutter would be used for these purposes as it minimizes damage. Also, it is recommended to apply a cut paste to the wound to aid the tree in healing as well as to stave off disease.

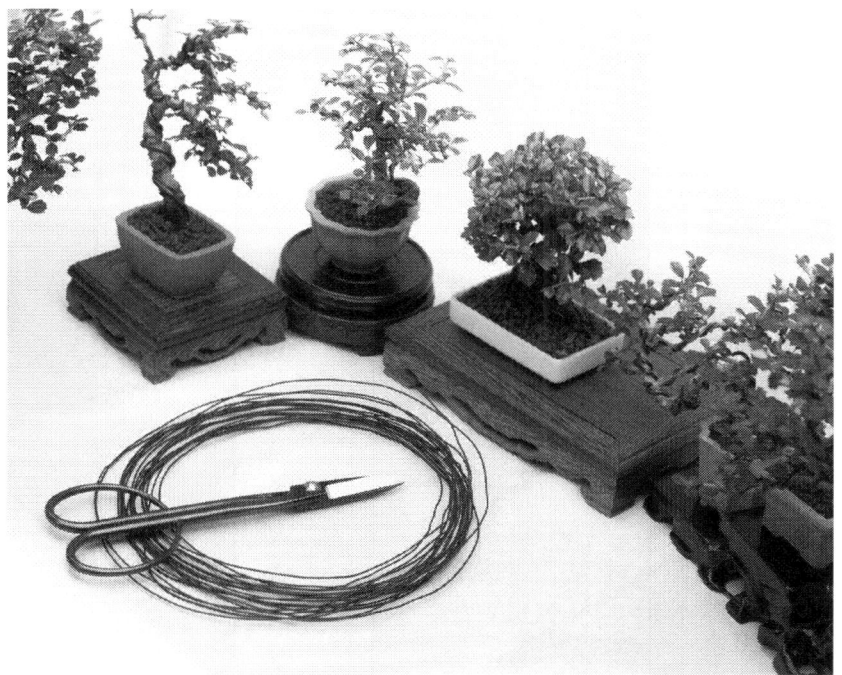

Wiring

When you want to reshape the branches, there is the option of wiring and securing the branches to create the final visual. This involves using various wires of aluminum, copper and guy wires. The first two are good choices for any tree. The guy wires, however, are highly recommended for beginners as they will not cut into the bark as much if you do not remove them in time.

Wiring is a technique that will probably be utilized at some point during the life of your bonsai. It is wire there is a section of wire which is wrapped around individual branches so they can bend in a specific direction. It takes at least three months for these effects to take effects. Close attention must be exercised while using wires as they easily can cut into branches which will cause sometimes permanent scarring. Before this occurs, the wires should be removed and rewired if required to retain or reshape the bonsai. This is particularly true during the growing seasons as the limbs can grow thick quickly.

The beautiful part about wiring is that most bonsais are able to be wired throughout the year. The ideal time for deciduous varieties is to perform the wiring in the late winter as the leaves have fallen. This makes it easier to access the branches and reduces the possibility of damaging leaves as they are not in the way during the process.

There are two main types of wires that can be used for bonsais which are anodized aluminum and annealed copper. The aluminum is what is used for the deciduous bonsais where the copper is used for the pines and conifers. As a beginner, it is acceptable to use aluminum for any type of bonsai as it is much easier to work with and hone your wiring skills.

You can get these wires in thicknesses ranging from 1 to 8 mm. It is recommended that you purchase thicknesses of 1 mm, 1.5 mm, 2.5 mm and 4 mm wire to have the variety that you require. If you are wrapping thicker branches then soak raffia, a palm fiber, in water to make it flexible. Wrap the raffia over the branch you want to wire and then twist the wire as desired. This protective layer keeps the branch from getting damaged as you are wrapping and bending the limb.

Wiring takes practice to master, but it does become a handy skill while working with your bonsai tree. There are two main ways in which wiring is applied known as single and double wiring. The wires are arranged on the branch before the bending process occurs which trains the limb to grow in a certain position.

Single Wiring Directions

You will need a length of wire which is 1/3 the thickness of the branch. Start by wrapping the wire around the trunk at a 45° angle twice as well as the branch in question. You want to arrange the wire loosely yet firmly in place, continuing at a 45° angle.

Double Wiring Directions

The branches that you want to bind together must be close together as well as similar in thickness. Cut off a section of wire which will wrap around the trunk twice as well as both of the branches. Arrange the wire around the trunk at a 45° angle which will aid in the wiring not moving as you manipulate the branches at a later time.

Then start to wrap the first branch while continuing with the 45° angle. Start from where the limb meets the trunk and go to the very end of the branch before performing the same on the other branch working from the tip to the trunk.

The exception to this style of wrapping is if you plan on bending the branch down at the trunk, the wiring needs to come from below. The opposite is true is the intention is to bend the limb upwards as the wire should be upwards.

After the double branches are complete, continue to wrap the other limbs using the single wiring directions.

If the entire tree is to be wrapped, start with the primary branches first before moving onto the secondary branches. Adjust the thickness of the wire depending on the section of the limb that is being wrapped. Refrain from crossing the wires over each other and use wire cutters to slice the wire.

Bending Techniques

After the process of wrapping the branches that you want to bend are complete, you start with the method of bending to manipulate the branches to the position you wish for them to be.

Grip the end of the branch you want to bend and then use your fingers, on the other hand, to push up or down on the weak bend in the branch to give it some leverage. Move the limb into the desired position and repeat the process for any other limbs. While you are going through this process, try to eliminate straight areas in the branch by bending the straight sections slightly. This will ultimately make your bonsai look more natural.

After the bonsai tree has been satisfactorily bent into shape, move the plant to the shade and feed with the normal fertilizer. Again, keep an eye on the wires, especially during the growing season and remove before damage occurs. Clip the wire in each curl to remove in small sections and discard.

Guy Wires

There is another technique that is helpful when the branches of the bonsai are too fragile or may break too easily while going through the wiring process. The method of guy wires puts less pressure on the branches yet still has the same result as wiring and bending the branch into place.

First, you want to cut a 2 inch (5 mm) section of 8 mm wire. You are going to create a sharp bend which will go over the limb. Place a piece of cloth or water-soaked raffia over the bending point of the limb.

Cut a 1–1.5 mm section of wire to the length required between the branch and the side of the container or root. Connect the thinner and thicker wire together and attach. Pull the wire as tightly as desired or before the branch is in danger of becoming damaged.

As is the case with the wiring, close attention must be given to make sure that the pressure of the wires to do not allow to cut into the bark of the limb. Otherwise, it will cause an unnatural dent or scar in the bark which will be there permanently.

Special Pruning and Wiring Guidelines of Certain Varieties

Adenium Bonsai

This bonsai is able to be pruned throughout the year. It is best to prune before the flower buds develop as this helps to create more buds as they appear on new shoots. Cut the shoots at a junction or leaf node and be sure to remove the damaged parts. Remember to utilize thick gloves when pruning as the milky sap is poisonous.

Remember while wiring the branches to not wrap them too tight. This will allow them to grow thicker without having to re-wire due to the wire cutting into the bark.

Azalea Bonsai

The pruning of the azalea bonsai is different from other bonsai types as the branches on the lower part of the plant are stronger on the base of the trunk. It is very accepting of hard pruning, and it is necessary to remove more of the bottom branches rather than the top. The timing of pruning is best during the spring months as well as during the summer after the flowers have wilted.

Remove the remaining flower peters and the ovaries by hand by pinching. This is a second opportunity to do any cleaning up of the azalea through a second trimming as necessary. Be sure not to prune the azalea any later than June as you will run the risk of having little or no flowers the next year. As an exception, the shoots at the base of the shrub can be removed at any time of the year without consequence.

If any wiring is required, it will take great care as the branches can be damaged easily. Use guy wires if you decide that bending and wiring is necessary.

Bald Cypress Bonsai

New shoots need to be shorted in early spring. This tree develops many new buds on the forks, branches, and trunk. If the buds are not needed for the overall design, remove them as soon as possible. Juvenile twigs and branches can be wired and shaped as the more mature branches become too brittle to be bent with damage occurring. Use guy wires and remove early so they do not bite in the branches, causing scarring.

Bougainvillea

After this bonsai flowers, prune the shoots while leaves two leaves on each and then cut the branches and twigs during the fall or winter months. This tree is able to produce buds of the mature branches even after hard pruning. If flowers are desired, do not trim back too much during the summer. However, when the flowers wilt, remove them before they cause issues with rot. It is recommended to use the cut paste on the larger wounds as they heal very slowly.

Wiring can be done when the twigs and shoots are in the juvenile stage but the mature branches break easily. Use protective gloves to keep your hands from being harmed from the thorns.

Boxwood Bonsai

When the canopy becomes very dense, thin out the leaves to allow breathability and light to be able to reach the inner twigs. Trim back the new shoots to have only two pairs of leaves. This bonsai responds well to heavy pruning and extensive sculpturing of the deadwood.

When wiring this bonsai, take special care not the damage the fragile bark as the scars will last for a very long time.

Brazilian Rain Tree Bonsai

Avoid die-back by leaving a small stub when this bonsai is pruned. When cutting back, do not use a concave cutter. Prune the shoots on a regular basis. When wanting to wire the branches, be sure to use guy wires and remove before they dig into the flesh.

Brush Cherry Bonsai

This shrub grows rather fast and needs to be cut back frequently. After eight pairs of leaves have grown, prune back to two leaves. Avoid making large branch cuts as wounds do not heal well.

Wiring can be done when cautious and mindful of the bark and branches as they are fragile. The ideal time to wire is during the growing season. Monitor the wire to remove before it scars the branches. Take your time to separate the wire as it is easy to break the branches when it is being removed.

Chinese Elm Bonsai

The foliage of this tree grows thick quickly, so pruning is encouraged regularly. However, any heavy pruning should be done during the fall months when bulky branches can be removed as well. Let the shoots grow to 4 nodes and then prune back to only two leaves. The Chinese elm can also be shaped rather easily with regular wires.

Chinese Pepper Bonsai

Do not ever remove all the leaves on the Chinese pepper. Prune back new shoots after four leaves are visible and cut back to two leaves. Wiring can be conducted throughout the year and guy wires are helpful with this bonsai to create the popular look of this plant.

Citrus Bonsai

When four leaves have developed, but back the shoots to have only two leaves. Regular pruning is important throughout the year.

Wiring should be performed with guy wires and can be done any time during the year. Ensure the wires are removed before damaging the bark on the branches.

Crepe Myrtle Bonsai

Pruning should occur at the end of summer as this will help the crepe myrtle to produce buds for the next year. Extreme caution should be used if wiring this bonsai as the bark surface is brittle. Use tape or wrap the paper around the wires that are wrapped around the branches and ensure they are removed in time to not bite the bark. It is recommended to use guy wires with this type of bonsai.

Ficus Bonsai

The Ficus trees need frequent pruning to keep the desired shape. It is recommended to remove 2 leaves after approximately 8 have grown. The pruning process can also be used to alter the size of the leaves depending on the schedule you prune. If the caretaker cares for a thick trunk, leave the tree to grow for between one to two years until the desired effective results. This variety of Bonsai trees heal rather well while new shoots will grow from pruned branches. If there are large wounds, the cut paste should be applied to the area.

Considering the branches are rather flexible, it is easy for the caregiver to manipulate the shape of the tree how they wish by utilizing guy-wires. Even though this type of wire can be in place for longer periods of time, monitoring is required to ensure that the wire does not cut into and damage the trunk or branches.

Flame Tree Bonsai

The pruning period is during the early spring months where they can be heavily cut without dire consequences. During the summer they must be frequently trimmed as they grow rather quickly. When the winter months come, remove the extra shoots which are needed for the next growing season.

If there is any requirement for wiring, plan these during the juvenile stage for the best results. If the flame tree is wired too late, they are very sensitive to damage from the wires growing into the bark.

Fukien Tea Bonsai

Consistent trimming is favorable to the Fukien Tea tree and will probably result in a dense branch structures. It is easier to wire supplier juvenile branches and twigs as the mature branches are quite brittle yet hard making binding a challenge.

Gardenia Bonsai

The gardenia bonsai should be pruned after it has flowered. If not fruits are not developing, cut away the withered flowers. The ideal time to wire the twigs and branches is during May and June as they are more pliable.

Ginkgo Bonsai

When the shoots have produced six leaves, cut them back to two leaves during the spring and summer. Try not to make any major branch cuts as large would do not heal well. If necessary, use cut paste on these wounds.

Wiring can occur throughout the year, but great care must be given to make sure that the branches and twigs are not damaged as the bark is very soft. Keep monitoring to remove the wires as soon as necessary to prevent injury.

Hawaiian Umbrella Bonsai

When the pruning of this bonsai is well thought out, there will be great results. Be sure If defoliation is performed, it will result in many new shoots and also with smaller leaves.

Wiring is a challenge for this tree and is best performed which the shoots are juvenile and bendable. Because the branches are fragile, it is advised not to wire any mature sections for fear of them breaking off.

Jade Bonsai

Pruning is encouraged with this plant regularly to encourage the bonsai to grow more branches lower on the trunk. Refrain from using the cut paste as it will lead to rotting. Wiring is rarely needed with this tree as the branches naturally bend from the water weight of the foliage.

Jarcaranda Bonsai

The soil of the Jacaranda needs to remain slightly wet. If the plant is not receiving enough water, the leaves will shrivel, turn brown and fall off the tree. If it is over-watered, the leaves will turn yellow and all fall off the bonsai.

Liquid fertilizer is recommended for this bonsai. It should be applied once a week during the growing season and twice a month during the winter months.

Japanese Cherry Bonsai

This plant should only be pruned during the spring. It is rather difficult to shape and may not be suited for the casual beginner. If the blossoms are desired, the bonsai should not be pruned for a whole year.

Japanese Elm Bonsai

When there are about six leaves, prune to leave only two leaves. Once the foliage falls, cut back the long shoots and twigs. With the younger trees, it is best to wait until June to remove the foliage. For older trees, it is recommended to discard the larger leaves so that more light and air may reach the inner foliage.

If the caretaker decides to use wires on their Japanese elm, it is ideal to perform these bonds before the buds open during every season except summer. Since the juvenile branches usually grow haphazardly, the caregiver will need to dedicate time to binding the limbs in a way that suits the final result they desire. Any wiring that was put into place needs to be discarded before the buds open in the spring.

Japanese Holly Bonsai

Prune as required throughout the year. If you desire flowers and fruit to form, stop cutting early in the summer. New shoots should be cut back to two leaves when four leaves have been developed.

Wiring is ideal during the late spring to summer. Bending of the branches need to be done with care as they are fragile. Use guy wires to protect the bark of the branches from scarring by removing before they bite the bark.

Japanese Maple Bonsai

Pruning is able to happen year-round; however, the branches which are strong should be cut only during the summer and fall which will keep the damage to the tree at a minimum. When you do prune, utilize the cut paste to ward off fungal diseases which are common at wound sites.

When the caregiver chooses to prune the Japanese Maple, be sure to keep it to no more than two pairs of leaves. If desired, you can choose to shape the twigs by using guy wiring. If the caregiver wishes to have smaller leaves, the pruning of the leaves should be completed during the early summer months.

Japanese Winterberry Bonsai

Because this bonsai uses the foliage to create energy to produce the fruit, do not ever remove all of the leaves by defoliation. Instead, prune back the shoots from four to two leaves. Wiring can be done any time other than the summer months as the leaves are fragile and will fall off easily when manipulating the branches to secure the wiring.

Juniper Bonsai

Refrain from pruning the Juniper Bonsais like hedges as the removal of the tips of the needles with weakening the entire tree resulting in the foliage turning brown. Ideally, the caregiver will clip the long shoots at the base of the branches to keep the foliage from becoming too dense. Even though the Junipers withstand much pruning measures, keep in mind that the branches do not bud again from wounds. To keep the branches from dying out, ensure there are some leaves left on the branches you want to preserve.

Often times when you purchase a Juniper Bonsai, it already has several wires in place since this is done at the time the tree is still a juvenile. This is due to the fact that Junipers are able to bent in extreme ways which result in the very popular visual seen with this variety of Bonsai. As an extra precaution, tape or raffia is used in combination with the wiring to minimize damage to the tree. This main precaution when shaping these plants is to pay attention to the deadwood as it will break easily if the caregiver manipulates this part of the Bonsai.

If the Juniper Bonsai is allowed to get too dense, the inner foliage will die as they are not able to receive the air or light they require. To solve this problem, the outside branches should be secured in a way that allows the leaves to be fanned. Once this has been completed, the tree will have a lessened chance of infestation from pests.

Money Tree Bonsai

Heavily prune this bonsai in the late winter months as it will respond in kind during the spring. It can be cut back to only two or three pairs of leaves.

Myrtle Bonsai

After the plant has flowered, cut back the new shoots to a pair of leaves when eight pairs of leaves are developed. When cutting larger branches, be sure to use cut paste on the wounds to quicken healing time and minimizing scarring. Wiring is only possible for juvenile branches as the more mature branches are too brittle and will break.

Oak Bonsai

When binding this tree, utilize guy wire and keep a close on the eye as it grows. The scars that are left if the wire damages in the trunk and/or limbs will last for some time.

Pruning should be conducted on in the early spring before the buds open. Trim the foliage back to only two leaves for the new shoots. If you keep up removing the large leaves, there will be no need to do major pruning. Also, take note that the foliage on the top of the Oak bonsai is much stronger than the ones located on the bottom branches.

Pine Bonsai

During the early to middle of summer, cut the candles of healthy bonsais so that only 5 mm remains. Remove the tip of the dormant buds to ensure their growth. Once the second round of growth has occurred in the fall, take off the excess shoots. If there are more than two shoots growing from one node, chose the two that are growing laterally and in a visually appealing way and form a "V" out of the shoots while removing the other shoots. Remove the needles where it is too thick to balance out the look of the tree.

If wiring is necessary, the ideal time to perform the binding is early in the spring, after the first cutting of the candles or early in the fall.

Olive Bonsai

Pruning is ideal during the late winter months. It is very forgiving and will grow back quickly in the spring. As a maintenance measure, prune back two or three pairs of leaves. If the tree is very full of foliage, you can practice defoliation on the bonsai to ensure the inside branches are receiving enough sunlight.

Redwood Bonsai

Any and all buds that are in excess need to be removed right away. Long twigs with internodes need to be cut during the spring before the flower buds open. This bonsai will create man new buds from the pruning scars. Working with the branches while wiring is a challenge because they are very fragile and subject to break. Use guy wires if you need to secure the branches.

Spruce Bonsai

Be sure to prune the spruce to have only one branch on the lower section of the tree so there are not several branches at the same level. During the spring, remove the new shoots by pinching off. Plan ahead when pruning as the tree will not bud from mature wood. Shorten the long branches and twigs.

Bending and wiring the branches is very possible with the spruce as the branches will not break. Naturally, the branches will bend due to them being used to carrying the weight of snow. Wiring will be a process which takes several years as the branches will remember their original position for some time. This means that wires will need to be used in several phases.

You can wire any time of the year except during the middle of the summer as it has the risk of dieback. The ideal times for wiring are during the early spring or late summer.

Weeping Willow Bonsai

During the winter time, remove the extra shoots that are not required. The caregiver can also cut the branches while leaving either one or two buds in anticipation for new growth during the spring. During the summer, it is necessary to cut the new shoots constantly.

Wiring should be completed during the month of June but keep an eye on this as you want to remove the wires when they are in danger of biting into the bark causing damage. For the older trees, the caregivers can secure the mature branches during the spring months.

Wisteria Bonsai

Major pruning should be reserved until the time after the Wisteria is flowering or early in the springtime. Once the foliage falls, the caregiver is able to cut back the twigs and branches in anticipation of binding the branches to the desired effect. Keep from pruning the short branches which will have flower buds. The younger plants are more keen on being pruned compared to the older vines.

The wisteria bonsai will get rather thick foliage that can be carefully pruned to remove leaves to bring more light and air to the inner foliage, but a caregiver never wants to completely remove the leaves from the vine. Keep the number of seed pods to the necessary minimum as they take valuable nutrients away from the remaining sections of the wisteria plant.

Chapter Summary

In this chapter, we learned

- There are several types of deciduous, broadleaf evergreens, conifers, and pines which can be used to create your own bonsai tree.
- Looking at the different needs of these trees should help in the ultimate decision process.
- Knowing the basics of the available options for trees should help you to choose which one is right for you
- In the next chapter, you will learn there is a broad range of insects, fungus and pests which attack bonsais. It will teach you how to monitor, detect and remedy pests, infections, and diseases.

CHAPTER SIX

PESTS, INFECTIONS, AND DISEASE REMEDIES

The first step in curbing pests and diseases is to monitor the bonsai tree regularly. If you start to have this problem, it is best to catch it as soon as possible. There are ways that would give you an indication that something is wrong with the tree if you happen to not notice issues upon inspection.

First of these signs being the leaves. If you notice that the leaves are wilting or turning brown or yellow, this is a big indication. Also, the leaves could start being covered in spots, holes or fall off the tree altogether. As a note, the leaves can have these same issues even without diseases or pests being present. Look for changes in the environment or maintenance routine to get to the root of the problem.

Other signs that your tree might be subject to pests is that the tree is not growing as fast as usual or there may be creamed colored larvae in the soil or on the tree itself. More evidence of pests is that there is a sticky residue left on the tree. The more obvious is when red spider mites attack your bonsai when you see webbing in between the leaves or branches. This pest is especially important to look for when the bonsai is a juniper.

If you find that your bonsai tree is infected, this is where you take a closer work. This is where it can get tricky, especially if the infection is in the roots. Once you have pinpointed the culprit, there are a few methods that generally can be followed to treat the bonsai tree from the infection or infestation.

1. Any leaves that have become diseased or infected should be removed to ensure it does not spread to other areas of the bonsai.

2. In the case of the leaves that have fallen off of an infected or infested tree, dispose of them carefully so that they will not continue to spread.

3. The tree should be relocated to a place that is secluded from any other plants to make sure the infestation or infection spreads to other plants.

4. A fungicide that is specific to the cause should be used as per the instructions.

5. If present, pests, and insects can be removed by hand picking them off of the tree or spraying with a water hose.

6. If the bonsai tree is located outside, another alternative may be to introduce healthy ladybugs which will eat most insects.

7. A mild solution of soap and water or a specific insect soap can be used to wash the pests away from the tree.

8. Any remaining insects and pests can be treated with an insecticide particular to the infestation. This can be sprayed directly onto the leaves or combined with the soil.

9. All tools used for the bonsai that has become infected or infested need to be thoroughly sterilized. This can be done with rubbing alcohol or disinfectant.

10. If a fungal infection is present, the soil should be removed and discarded away from the property. It is not to be used again by any other plant for fear of the infection continuing to live in the soil.

11. If you decide to use the container again, it needs to be scrubbed and washed thoroughly before being used again.

12. The bonsai tree should be moved to a place which has good ventilation.

Treatment of Specific Pests and Insects

Red Mites

These very small insects can lead to the death of your bonsai. They are usually located on the bottom of the leaves and can easily be missed unless closely inspected. Sometimes evidence of their presence can be seen when there is a very fine web located on the foliage.

One foolproof way of checking is to just a white sheet of paper. Hold the paper underneath a branch as you lightly tap the branch. If the red mites are present, they will fall on the paper, making them more noticeable. The recommended treatment is to use an organic insect soap or insecticide and apply directly to the underside of the foliage.

Scale Insects

These are also a very small pest which is brown, white or yellow. They create a sticky substance which may be the first sign that you notice that your bonsai has been infested. Otherwise, this is a difficult insect to spot as they are usually located under the bark. Owners of Fukien Tea Bonsais need to monitor their tree for this type of pest.

The recommended treatment is to use your hands to remove the insects. Scales have a protective shell which is difficult to infiltrate making insecticides less effective as a sure treatment of their infestation. Also, because they are located under the bark, it is best when they move to other sections of the bonsai to pick them off the tree.

Vine Weevils

These pests are able to be seen easily when the adults lay their eggs into the soil. Like most pests, these weevils can create a lot of damage to your bonsai trees. When the eggs hatch, the larvae will attack and eat the roots of the tree, going undetected. One way of knowing there is a problem is that the leaves will start to wilt.

The recommended treatment is to use an insecticide to remove the adult insects so they can be prevented from laying more eggs. Then the plant will need to be re-potted in a new container and soil. As the tree is being transplanted, remove all larvae present to prevent an infestation from occurring again. As an added measure, the insecticide can be combined with the new soil.

Aphids

These insects are dangerous because they are able to multiply quickly. They are green or black flies which fasten themselves to the plant as they eat the sap of the trees. Because they are depleting the nutrients from the bonsai, the tree will start showing signs of infection by displaying weak branches and leaves that will curl. One way to notice that these aphids are present are they leave a sugary substance known as honeydew on the foliage. This substance can result in the formation of mold.

Treatment recommendations are to use the soapy water solution or a specific insecticide spray. Like all infestations, it needs to be treated as soon as possible.

Caterpillars

This pest is much easier to notice because of their size. Also because they will leave obvious holes in the foliage of the bonsai tree. They are able to cause a decent amount of damage in a short period, especially if there are several.

The best treatment that is recommended is to remove the caterpillars by hand. To ensure they all have been removed, you can couple insect spray with the treatment.

Mealy Bugs

Being a silent pest, they can start to feed on the root system in addition to being under the branches and leaves themselves. They have white balls like cotton in which they hide in clusters. The best-recommended treatment is to use contact insecticide or use a systematic spray.

Slugs and Snails

These pests are dormant except when the temperature is 50° Fahrenheit (10° Celsius) during the spring months. They are able to be noticed because of their size or by the slimy trails they secrete. The treatment that is recommended is to take them off the tree by hand. If the bonsai is located outdoors, the use of slug bait can be an effective way to ensure they will infest the tree again.

Treatment of Specific Diseases and Infections

Root Rot

This is a common issue which occurs when there is too much moisture retained in the soil. This happens usually when a heavy soil such as peat is being used, the plant is being watered too often or there are not enough drainage holes in the container. The longer this condition remains, the more chance there is that the roots will start to deteriorate. This affects the entire tree as it starts to lose nutrients and the foliage will probably turn brown. You may also press against the trunk and it feels soft. If not treated, the entire bonsai will die. In the case of under watering, this can occur in a matter of days. It takes a few weeks for the roots to rot if you have been overwatering your bonsai.

The best treatment is removing the roots that are affected by pruning them away from the good roots. Then transplant the tree into another container with proper drainage holes. Use soil which drains well. Follow the watering recommendations found in chapter seven about proper hydration of your bonsai tree to prevent this from happening again. Discard the soil as it may still have the infection present.

Rust

This is an infection that will be noticed on the underside of the foliage. It appears as a small raised section which can be a range of colors between brown, red, orange or yellow. Another indication is that the leaves will start to curl and then fall off of the bonsai tree. The best way to control this infection is to prune the affected leaves before they spread further.

Leaf Spot

This is a type of fungal infection which has stages. The first thing that will be observed is there will be white spots which appear on the foliage. During the next stage of the infection, the color of the spots changes to gray, brown or black. In the final stages of infection, the affected leaves will fall off the tree. The treatment is to remove the infected leaves off of the tree and then apply a spray fungicide over the entire tree.

Black Spot

This is a virus which affects the foliage of the bonsai trees, especially the Chinese Elm. The result of this virus is that the leaves turn yellow and then they fall off of the tree. The recommended treatment is to prune the infected leaves and then treat the complete tree with a spray fungicide.

Mildew

When the tree is located in damp conditions, this fungus will probably thrive. White powder will be noticeable and present on the foliage and cannot be removed simply by brushing the powder off the leaves. The treatment which is recommended is the leaves which are affected the need to be removed. The remaining foliage needs to be washed with water and soap as this fungus spreads by spores. This process may need to be repeated multiple times until the fungus has been completely removed.

Twig and Tip Blight

This disease occurs during warm weather and when the soil has retained too much moisture. The result of this disease is that the tips of the bonsai leaves will turn brown and then fall off of the tree. The recommended treatment is to remove the leaves that are affected and then use a disinfectant where the foliage was pruned to keep the disease from infecting other areas.

Other Common Issues

Chlorosis

This is the result of the incorrect amount of minerals being present in the soil. The nutrients in question are iron, manganese, and magnesium. This is commonly seen in bonsais that the soil requires a higher acidic content such as Azaleas. Determine the current levels of the mineral present in the soil and combine the correct amount of nutrients for your particular bonsai tree.

Dieback

When your bonsai tree is stressed out, it reacts by dropping the leaves that are not needed for the survival of the tree. This may result in some or most of the leaves falling. This issue occurs for several reasons including an infestation of pests or insects, the location of the tree, root rot or improper watering. Determine the underlying cause of the stress and act accordingly.

Mold

This is the result of an infestation of insects, likely aphids, that excrete honeydew onto the leaves. If this sugary substance is allowed to stay on the leaves, it will turn into a black residue that can be rubbed off by hand. The treatment required is to prune the leaves that are affected so the mold will not spread. Gently hand-wash the leaves with a mixture of soap and water to remove the residue. Repeat the washing as necessary to remove the mold completely. Also, it is important to know that mold is spread through spores, so moving the plant into isolation is also a requirement.

Chapter Summary

This chapter covered the following aspects :

- What tasks to perform when you first notice the sign of an infestation.
- An overview of different types of pests, insects, and diseases which can plague bonsai trees.
- Informs you of how to create a healthy environment to keep your bonsai pest and disease free.
- Specific instructions on how to care and treat your bonsai when affected by pests, insects, and diseases.
- In the next chapter, you will learn about the common mistakes that all beginners make and how to fix these problems. Learn how to water your bonsai properly and how to ensure that you are caring for your bonsai in the best way possible.

CHAPTER SEVEN

COMMON MISTAKES & REMEDIES

There are certain guidelines to follow which will ensure that your bonsai will last for years if not generations to come. Sometimes new owners think that the bonsai trees will grow well on their own and they will only need to prune them as needed. However, taking care of a bonsai is a dedicated practice.

Proper Watering

The biggest mistake that is made with new bonsai owners is that they do not properly water their tree. People will treat their bonsai like any other plant and water it accordingly. However, bonsai trees are particular about the watering schedule. It is possible to under or over water the tree, and there are many consequences that can arise when the moisture in the soil is not the correct balance. If the roots have not completely dried out, they are able to be saved by following the proper watering guidelines for your type of bonsai.

The role of water is important for any plant or tree. This is due to the leaves using nutrients and water to convert the energy from the sunshine and through the process of photosynthesis to create the sugars required to grow. Over 55% of the weight of the bonsai is water, and it aids in the nutrients being transported to the entire tree. The majority of this water is taken in by the root system. This is why watering and keeping the roots from rotting are the number one way to keep your bonsai thriving.

The way to determine the amount of water required is to first look at the type of soil that is being used. As a rule of thumb, most bonsais need to be watered when the soil becomes dry slightly. You do not want the soil to dry out or be waterlogged. Both of these instances will result in root rot. This is an important step because if it is not followed, it is possible to damage a bonsai beyond repair within a week's time.

To properly water your bonsai, only water when the soil is a little dry. If you press your finger into the dirt along the edge of the pot, you can test the moisture content of the soil. Press until the soil starts to become moist to determine the amount of water that is needed to moisten the dirt. Alternatively, a moisture gauge can be purchased to have a more precise measurement of the water content of the soil before adding more.

Water the tree and then wait a 3–4 minutes. Water again to ensure that all the soil has been moistened. Another way to know that you have watered it enough is when the water is draining through the holes in the base of the container. If you own a smaller potted tree, it is best to use a spray bottle as any large amount of water is going to wash away the soil from the root system.

It may be necessary during the spring and summer months to water daily if not twice a day depending on the type of bonsai and the climate. For example, if you have a bonsai which is a deciduous or flowers, it will need more water. However, some varieties will only require water once a week. During other times of the year when the bonsai is not in the growing season, it will require less water. Be sure to test to the soil to know for sure what your particular bonsai needs.

Every month, set the bonsai into a bucket of water so that the water can be drawn from the base of the container. Leave it for only 20 minutes and then move the pot back to its original location. Always lift your bonsai by the pot and not the tree itself.

Proper Soil

If you purchased a cheap Chinese bonsai, it likely came with clay-based soil. This is not ideal for the bonsai as most of the water will not be absorbed into the dirt but rather rest on the base of the container or has drained out of the pot. If your bonsai is in clay, transfer as soon as possible with soil suited for your variation of bonsai tree. Usually, this is a loose and gravel combination.

Bonsais do not grow well in potting soil and it should be avoided. There are specific blends available for bonsais which usually contain small particles which allow for the aeration of the soil as the roots require oxygen to function properly.

Fertilization is a key component for the soil. It needs to be combined with the soil during the growing season starting in the early spring months through the middle of the fall. The need for fertilization is required because of the nature of the shallow pots that bonsais are commonly planted. The roots are able to stretch out which searching for more nutrients during the growing season. However, they are not able to stretch far because of the limited space. This is why you need to replenish the nutrients in the soil as your bonsai grows.

The mature bonsais do not need to be fertilized as often. Bonsais located indoors can be fertilized throughout the year. However, if you have transplanted your bonsai, keep the soil fertilizer free for approximately a month as your bonsai adjusts to the new environment. If your tree happens to be sick, do not fertilize the soil. This may actually exasperate the illness as they are likely not able to process the nutrients properly, resulting in nutrient burn.

There are three macronutrients that are required by bonsais known as the NPK ratio. These components are nitrogen, phosphorus, and potassium. The purpose of the nitrogen is to help the stems, branches, and leaves to grow. The phosphorus is a requirement for the development of healthy roots and also plays a part in the production of fruits and flowers. Finally, potassium is needed for the overall health of the tree. It is important to find the particular combination of the NPK ratio that is required for your variety of bonsai tree as it changes throughout the year.

Proper Sunlight

Sunlight is very important as they will require an ample amount of sunlight. The best idea is to find a well-ventilated area that is in the direct sunlight whether indoors or outdoors. If you find a south-facing window indoors, this will be the ideal spot for the bonsai tree.

Indoor or Outdoor Bonsai?

There are certain types of bonsai trees that are designed to be indoors and likewise outdoors. If a tree is bred to be an indoor bonsai, it cannot be placed in an outdoor garden and vice versa. It is best to ask the seller before you decide on which bonsai to purchase. However, if you are not sure what type your particular tree is, you will probably notice after a short period as the tree will start to show signs of stress. This is seen when the leaves will discolor or fall off for "no reason" or that the tree itself seems to not be growing to its full potential.

It is beneficial as well to mimic the same environment as the location where the tree was obtained. This will create a healthy space for the bonsai tree to grow and it will put the bonsai through less shock as it will seem like the natural environment to the tree, even if you bought it from Asia.

Too Many Modifications

Even though it is part of the maintenance of owning a bonsai tree to keep pruning it throughout the year. Pruning is necessary to bring extra sunlight to the inner branches, but you can cut away too much which will leave your bonsai unable to gather the nutrients required from the sunlight.

However, when you want to reshape the tree, only do this once a year. This is due to the bonsai trees being sensitive and they need time to recover from these changes. Think of it as an operation where recuperation time is required. This also includes other major changes such as repotting the tree as it can cause a shock if done too many times in a short period.

Wrong Size Container

When you first purchase a bonsai, the size of the plant is also an important aspect that needs great care and attention. You cannot just select any pot for your bonsai as they need to be the correct shape and size and even color for your particular bonsai tree. The first aspect of container selection is to consider the root system. The pot needs to be large enough for the roots to be able to stretch slightly so it has space to grow until it is time to transplant. This also gives the roots the room they require gathering the nutrients and water from the soil.

Another aspect of container selection is the size of your bonsai and the root system. Do you want to keep the bonsai at the current size or do you want it to continue to grow? Is your tree more mature and grown to the size you wish it to be? If so, you would transfer it to another pot of similar size and shape as you are going to be pruning the root system each time it is re-potted. If you want it to still grow in size, place it in a slightly larger pot according to the desired final result. The perfect sized pot is one which is slightly smaller in width than the longest branches.

Incorrect Tools

Severe and irreparable damage can occur if a gardener is using incorrect tools for their bonsai maintenance and care. Every bonsai owner should own a pair of high-quality bonsai scissors. These are a specialty tool created for properly pruning bonsais with as little damage as possible. They are made to cut through wires which are supporting your tree as well as branches. If you utilize regular scissors for these tasks, it will end up damaging your bonsai and likely cause scarring.

You will also need to have branch cutters, wire pliers and wire cutters the more mature your bonsai becomes. These are all tools which will need to be specifically for bonsai tree care and the maintenance of your tree will grow more complex as the tree matures.

Be sure to care for your tools and keep them in the best shape possible. To remove rust or dirt from the blades, you can use a product known as Clean Mate. To keep the tools sharp, purchase a grindstone as branches and leaves need to be sliced cleanly. This cannot happen with a dull pair of scissors or cutters and will, in turn, damage your bonsai.

For proper upkeep of the tools, they need to be disinfected periodically. This is a requirement if your bonsai has gone through any time of infection or infestation of pests. Also if you have more than one tree, then this will minimize the transfer of possible bacterial, virus and fungal infections.

Action Steps if your Bonsai is Dying

If you have found yourself where your tree is suffering and dying, there is some hope if you have caught the symptoms in time. There are guidelines to try to revive your bonsai tree. First, you need to know the type of tree and if it is an indoor or outdoor bonsai. This will help you to determine the specific needs and care for your particular tree. If you have not already, educate yourself on the particular type of bonsai you own as some variations have niche needs which may be the cause of the tree dying.

Ensure that you have followed the guidelines for the location, fertilization, and watering of your plant. If not, adjust accordingly. Sometimes this alone will bring the bonsai back to life when it is in its ideal environment to thrive.

Keep in mind that bonsais are better kept in temperatures greater than 20° Fahrenheit (-6° Celsius) during the winter time. You can bring them inside to a warmer place as the bonsai does not need sunlight while in a dormant state. You may notice the foliage turn brown, but they will become green again during the spring when they are set back outside.

Make sure that your bonsai tree is supposed to be indoors or outdoors. As an example, the popular Juniper bonsais are an outdoor plant. If placed indoors, the foliage will start to yellow and fall off the tree. Because most of the indoor bonsais are sub-tropical trees, they require abundant light. Some new owners may think for this reason that it is best to keep their bonsai outdoors. However, the guidelines for each variety must be followed.

Once you are knowledgeable about the particular care for your variety of bonsai tree, continue to follow those guidelines as this is the best thing that can be done for your tree going forward to revive and thrive.

Chapter Summary

This chapter covered

- The biggest mistakes that are made by beginners including over and under watering and ensuring there is enough sunlight or shade.
- How to remedy the common mistakes made and how to hone your skills of bonsai care.
- Ways to revive your dying bonsai tree when the care guide has not been followed.
- In the next chapter, you will see a visual gallery of the different styles of bonsais. This will give you an idea of what style you would like to work towards for your chosen bonsai.

CHAPTER EIGHT

STYLE GUIDE

There are several common styles that are used for bonsais. Here is a visual guide which will help you to know the end result of your bonsai.

Kengai

Known as the cascading style, the trunk of this Bonsai tree grows straight and then branches swoops abruptly downward. The visual is to represent a tree on a mountainside.

Chokkan

This is an upright and formal Bonsai style which is what the original style which Bonsai trees are based upon. These bonsai trees are styled to reach their limbs towards the sky with no particular angle in mind. This a style which can be complicated to perfect as it is ruined if any branch of this tree dies.

Yose-ue

A type of group planting, the Yose-ue Bonsai are several plants which are growing in a shallow pot and are produced from many groups of roots. The visual representation is of groves or forests found in nature. This is a complex style according to the new rules of the art of the bonsai. However, in traditional times, artisans would use several plants lined in a row.

Shakan

This style takes on a slanting form as the branches are swept to one side. The visual associated with the Shakan is that of a tree in a storm or high wind. Because of this depiction, it is also known by the name of windswept.

Hokidachi

This style is known as a broom form because of the shape it takes. The Hokidachi is closely related to Chokkan because it is semi-formal and upright. What sets this tree apart is the branches do not climb straight up. Rather, they grow out in clusters. This tree takes the most time as it takes many years for this Bonsai to take the proper form. This makes the Hokidachi one of the most challenging Bonsai trees to have because of the skill and dedication required.

Moyogi

This is another upright style yet informal. The tree looks as if it is in motion due to the trunk and branches bending to the front of the Bonsai rather than straight.

Neagari

This style is characterized by exposed roots. The representation of the Neagari Bonsai tree is to symbolize the elements being washed away from the roots in nature.

Ishizuki

These Bonsai trees are formed around a rock. This style is a representation of when rocks and trees exist together in nature and find a balance to work together. This is a more advanced technique because most of the root system grows over the rock. The soil that is recommended for this type of style is clay which also makes the Ishizuki style more of a challenge.

Sokan

This is known as the Bonsai tree with twin trunks. The double trunks will come from one root system and there is larger, dominating trunk. A variation found in nature, this is the result of the climate and placement of the tree. The trunks usually form a "V" and they both come together to form one canopy.

Kabudachi

This is a Bonsai with five or more trunks. There is a main trunk which serves as the centerpiece of the other smaller trunks. They have a canopy in the shape of a triangle or slightly slanted towards the outward sections in a cascade fashion. This is an intermediate style as you are taking care of several bonsais in one.

FINAL WORDS

Thank you for purchasing your copy of *Bonsai: A Beginners Guide on How to Cultivate and Care for Bonsai Trees.* I hope that you enjoyed learning about this ancient art form and feel more confident in undertaking your new hobby.

If you follow the guidelines in this book, you will be successful in raising and creating your own unique piece of nature. You will understand how to deal with any problems that may come up and hopefully keep practicing bonsai sculpting.

If you found this book useful in any way, an honest review is always appreciated! Thank you!

40279854R10075

Made in the USA
San Bernardino, CA
26 June 2019